Philosophy and its Past

PHILOSOPHY NOW

General Editor: Roy Edgley

English-speaking philosophy since the Second World War has been dominated by the method of linguistic analysis, the latest phase of the analytical movement started in the early years of the century. That method is defined by certain doctrines about the nature and scope both of philosophy and of the other subjects from which it distinguishes itself; and these doctrines reflect the fact that in this period philosophy and other intellectual activities have been increasingly monopolised by the universities, social institutions with a special role. Though expansive in the number of practitioners, these activities have cultivated an expertise that in characteristic ways has narrowed their field of vision. As our twentieth-century world has staggered from crisis to crisis, English-speaking philosophy in particular has submissively dwindled into a humble academic specialism, on its own understanding isolated from the practical problems facing society, and from contemporary Continental thought.

The books in this series are united by nothing except discontent with this state of affairs. Convinced that the analytical movement has spent its momentum, its latest phase no doubt its last, the series seeks in one way or another to push philosophy out of its ivory tower.

Other books in the Series:

FREEDOM AND LIBERATION: *Benjamin Gibbs*
HEGEL'S PHENOMENOLOGY: *Richard Norman*
RULING ILLUSIONS: PHILOSOPHY AND THE SOCIAL ORDER:
   Anthony Skillen
ART AN ENEMY OF THE PEOPLE: *Roger Taylor*
THE WORK OF SARTRE: SEARCH FOR FREEDOM: *Istvan Meszaros*
THE POSSIBILITY OF NATURALISM: *Roy Bhaskar*
THE RISE OF WESTERN RATIONALISM: *P. Feyerabend*
THE DIALECTIC OF REVOLUTION: *C. J. Arthur*
SCIENCE AND IDEOLOGY: *Roy Edgley*

Philosophy
and its Past

JONATHAN RÉE
Lecturer in Philosophy, Middlesex Polytechnic
MICHAEL AYERS
Fellow of Wadham College, Oxford
ADAM WESTOBY
Lecturer, The Open University

THE HUMANITIES PRESS · NEW JERSEY

Published in USA by
HUMANITIES PRESS INC.
Atlantic Highlands, New Jersey 07716
First published by The Harvester Press, England

Library of Congress Cataloging in Publication Data

Rée, Jonathan, 1948—
    Philosophy and its past.

    (Philosophy now)
    Includes index.
    1. Philosophy—Historiography—Addresses, essays, lectures. 2.
Analysis (Philosophy)—Addresses, essays, lectures. 3. Hegel, Georg
Wilhelm Friedrich, 1770-1831—Addresses, essays, lectures. I. Ayers,
Michael Richard, joint author. II. Westoby, Adam, joint author. III.
Title. IV. Series.
B51.4.R4   190   77-13049

ISBN 0-391-00544-8

Typeset by
Cold Composition Ltd, Tonbridge, Kent
Printed in England by
Redwood Burn Ltd., Trowbridge & Esher

Contents

INTRODUCTION

Chapter One

PHILOSOPHY AND THE HISTORY OF PHILOSOPHY

Chapter Two

ANALYTICAL PHILOSOPHY AND THE HISTORY OF PHILOSOPHY

CONTENTS

Chapter Three

HEGEL'S HISTORY OF PHILOSOPHY

INTRODUCTION

Whether they are conscious of it or not, all disciplines have some sense of their own historical development. Though it may contain more myth than genuine historical knowledge, their sense of history is part of their intellectual credentials and of their definition of themselves. And philosophers take their sense of their disicpline's past much more seriously than, say, physicists or psychologists, usually seeing explicit study of the history of philosophy as an important element of the training in their discipline. But the 'history of philosophy' is a very peculiar kind of history. The historian Lucien Febvre writes as follows:

> Historians of philosophy?...Of all the people who lay claim to the title of historians...there are none, I believe, who are not in some way entitled to it, with the exception of those who try to rethink, on their account, systems of thought which may be several centuries old, without taking the slightest trouble to notice their relation to other phenomena of the period which gave rise to them and who therefore end up doing precisely the opposite of what the method of historians requires[1].

The paradox about histories of philosophy, then, is that they appear to have almost nothing to do with history.

The purpose of this collection of new essays is to explore the significance of this unhistorical history of philosophy. In my own chapter, I have examined the history of histories of philosophy and suggested that they are connected with the constitution of philosophy as a distinct academic subject. In the second chapter, Michael Ayers traces the effects of unhistorical ideas about the history of philosophy on some modern interpretations of philosophical classics. Both these chapters show a complex and close relationship between philosophical doctrines and ideas about the history of philosophy; and in the third chapter, on Hegel's *History of Philosophy*, Adam Westoby demonstrates this relationship in a particular case.

This collection does very little to answer the question how the history of philosophy ought to be written; in fact it raises the prior question of whether philosophy has a self-contained and continuous history at all. I hope it will help people to think effectively about these questions.

Jonathan Rée

[1]Lucien Febvre, *Combats pour l'histoire*, Paris, 1953, p278.

Chapter One

PHILOSOPHY AND THE
HISTORY OF PHILOSOPHY

by

Jonathan Rée

The History of Philosophy is and always has been part of philosophy; and philosophy is much more concerned with its past than any other modern academic discipline. (A philosophy student is expected to know something about Aristotle and Descartes, but a chemist might scarcely have heard of Lavoisier or Priestley, or a historian of Guicciardini or Ranke). But the History of Philosophy is not so much a self-conscious discipline as a conglomerate of unconscious philosophical and historical instincts. It is not history which just happens to be about philosophy. Histories of philosophy, whether surveys of the centuries or studies of individual philosophers, are not written by historians—not even cultural or intellectual historians or historians of ideas. Like histories of music, of the visual arts or of various literatures, histories of philosophy belong to a tradition with its own categories, methods and periodisation. But while histories of art are written by specialist art historians, not by artists, and histories of science by historians of science rather than by scientists, histories of philosophy are always written by philosophers— and indeed are not normally of much use or interest to anyone else.

The History of Philosophy depicts Ancient Greece, represented mainly by Plato and Aristotle; the Middle Ages, characterised by scholasticism and personified in Aquinas; and modern philosophy, dominated by rationalism, empiricism, idealism and materialism as expressed by Descartes, Spinoza, Leibniz, Locke, Hume and Kant. Normally averting its eyes from nineteenth-century thinkers, especially Marx[1], it tries to join twentieth-century philosophy directly to Kant. The historiographical and philosophical bases of this story have seldom been though about, let alone systematically criticised[2], but they are open to plenty of objections. Historians of philosophy project into the past an idea of philosophy as a professional academic specialism—treating Aristotle and Descartes as though they were participants at a modern philosophy conference, or even candidates in a philosophy exam; they do not explore historical sources other than explicitly philosophical writings; they do not know whether they should be concerned with *great* philosophy or with *influential* philosophy; they never consider general problems about the interpretation of philosophical texts; and they are so preoccupied with explicit controversies between philosophers that they fail to notice areas of agreement or of silence. Finally, their interpretations are false in countless ways: they not only attribute to people beliefs which were not theirs, but also, often, beliefs too nonsensical ever to have been held by anyone (see Chapter Two).

The History of Philosophy is not an optional appendix to philosophy. It identifies the main theories and controversies of philosophy; it canonises the great thinkers and the basic texts of the discipline; and it defines the chief tendencies and periods of its development. In this way, it provides an implicit definition of philosophy, indicating that being a philosopher means being a successor to Plato, Aristotle and the rest and perpetuating the practices which—according to the History of Philosophy—these Great Men have bequeathed. Of course, disagreements about the nature of philosophy remain. For instance, recent Western philosophers have put forward various rival definitions: philosophy is conceptual analysis, or the search for the ultimate presuppositions of systems of thought, or the theory of theoretical practice, or class struggle at the level of theory, and so on. But these definitions would not be rivals if they were not intended to be definitions of the same thing; and the identification of this 'same thing' is performed by the History of Philosophy. So its categories are not only applied retrospectively (and perhaps untruly) to the past. Its image of the past is translated into the reality of the present: the nature of modern philosophy is partly determined by the unexamined presuppositions of the History of Philosophy.

In what follows I attempt to identify and criticise these presuppositions by surveying the historical development of histories of philosophy. In Part One, I examine ideas concerning the *form* of philosophy—the nature of philosophical disagreements and of their resolution. In Part Two, I consider ideas concerning the subject matter or *content* of philosophy. Finally, in Part Three, I attempt to assess the function and effects of histories of philosophy.

Part One
Histories of Philosophy and the form of Philosophy: the idea of 'Warring Schools'

The Enlightenment: Brucker and the Philosophes
Renaissance thinkers saw themselves as moving away from the limited, monkish world view of medieval Christianity and took an unprecedented interest in history, especially the history of thought[3]. They divided history into three periods, ancient, middle and modern, describing the ancient age as a period of enlightenment and the middle age as a period of darkness. Their own task, as they saw it, was to break with the immediate past, and to study the ancient age in order to restore its values in a heroic modern age[4].

Amongst seventeenth century thinkers, idealisation of ancient Greece and Rome diminished; but the conviction that modern thinkers must reject the past, especially the middle age, remained. As a rule, they believed it was best to ignore past thinkers, ancient and medieval alike[5], especially as, in Descartes' words, 'they all say something different'[6]. Francis Bacon, it is true, considered it worthwhile to classify and record the doctrines of past thinkers, but this was not so much because he expected to find anything of value in them as because he thought everything should be classified and recorded[7]. For thinkers like Bacon, Descartes and Pascal, the antiquity of a doctrine was a reason for forgetting about it rather than for studying it. As Descartes said:

I do not see why we should give any respect to the antiquity of
the ancients. It would in fact be better to say that we are the
more ancient, since the world is older now than it was then[8].

But rejecting the past is not the same as having no sense of
history; on the contrary, it involves definite convictions about
the historical tasks of the present. And the seventeenth century
saw the first modern works which have any claim to be called
histories of pholosophy. Thomas Stanley's *History of
Philosophy*, which was supposed to be based on Baconian
principles, and which came out in 1655, was one such work.
Stanley began with 'Barbarian' (for example, Hebrew)
philosophy, and went on to describe the philosophy of ancient
Greece. But Stanley's account stopped at Jesus Christ, in
whom complete philosophical truth had supposedly been
revealed. In addition, Stanley's *History* was somewhat
fanciful—it is typical, for example, that his account of Plato
begins with a discussion of Plato's virgin birth—but in spite of
its faults it remained popular well into the nineteenth century[9].

Another and much fuller account of the development of
philosophy, by Georg Horn, was published in Holland in the
same year as Stanley's[10]. Like Stanley, Horn drew his
inspiration from Bacon. Horn's *History* was based on the old
theory that the whole of philosophy had been known to
Adam[11] and that the way back to the truth was indicated by the
Old Testament. In spite of its archaic framework, this was a
pioneering work because it took the story of thought right up
to the present[12].

The works of Stanley and Horn, however, were not really
histories of philosophy. As their dependence on religious
sources and notions shows, they were histories of thought in
general, rather than histories of philosophy as such. Histories
of philosophy, in this more narrow sense, did not appear until
the 'Enlightenment' of the eighteenth century. The crucial
work here was the *Critical History of Philosophy*[13], by Johann
Jakob Brucker, the fifth and last enormous volume of which
was published in Leipzig in 1744. Brucker began with an
account of Hebrew and Chaldean philosophy or 'philosophy
before the flood', in which he thoroughly criticised the idea that
Adam had known the whole of philosophy; next he gave an
admiring account of the Greeks; and then he explained the

decline of philosophy amongst the Romans, the Jews, the Arabs and the Christians, and ruefully described how sects had proliferated in the middle age. Finally he turned with relief to the modern age.

> Having at length, not without difficulty, cleared our way through the thorns and briars of the Middle Age, we are now arrived at more open and pleasant country, where we shall see learning and philosophy recovering their ancient honours...At length, genius was awakened, rational inquiry was resumed, and the night of the scholastic age was succeeded by a bright day of learning and true philosophy[14].

The modern age, according to Brucker, had seen 'The Restoration of Universal Eclectic Philosophy', medieval sectarianism having been supplanted by an open-mindedness or eclecticism similar to that which had prevailed in antiquity.

The philosophes, like Diderot, Voltaire, and Hume were scornful of Brucker's Lutheranism and of his inelegant prose, but they found most of their own ideas about philosophy expounded and industriously documented in his work. In fact most of Diderot's articles on the history of philosophy in the *Encyclopedia* were lifted from Brucker[15]. The philosophes shared Brucker's admiration for ancient philosophy, his dismissive concept of the middle ages[16], and his correspondingly complacent view of the modern age. Gibbon was being exceptionally generous when he observed that 'the darkness of the middle ages exhibits some scenes not unworthy of our notice'. Hume said that the philosophers of the middle ages were 'universally infected with superstition and sophistry' and believed that it was only in modern times that mankind had 'thrown off this yoke'. Voltaire, referring to the thirteenth century, remarked that the only progress had been 'from savage ignorance to scholastic ignorance'[17] and stated that the story of the middle ages was 'the barbaric history of barbaric peoples, who did not become any the better for becomng Christians'[18].

The enlightenment conception of the identity of modern as opposed to medieval thought was accompanied by the hardening of several other identities and separations. There was a growing assertion of the unity of the European traditions, particularly those of the Arabs, the Jews, the Chinese, and the Indians, all of whom were extensively discussed by Brucker. At the same time, the origins of philosophy came to be located in the pre-Socratic period in Ancient Greece rather than in the 'barbaric ages' before[19]. In addition, a definite, though still very broad, conception of philosophy as a distinct branch of thought was beginning to establish itself. Brucker's register of modern philosophers was divided into general philosophers and particular philosophers. In the first group he mentioned Bruno, Cardan, Bacon, Campanella, Hobbes, Descartes, Leibniz and others. He subdivided the second group, the particular philosophers, into three sections: first, Logic and Metaphysics, represented by Ramus, Arnauld and Spinoza; second, Morals and Politics, represented by Montaigne, Charron and Macchiavelli; and third, Natural Philosophy, represented by Copernicus, Tycho Brahe, Kepler, Galileo, Boyle and Newton. Thus although Brucker included the whole of theoretical natural science within the history of philosophy, he separated philosophy from religion and did not impose religious principles of classification or periodisation on it.

Updating the origin of philosophy and separating it from religion enabled Brucker and, following him, and philosophes, to enforce the most pervasive, most influential, but perhaps least conscious elements of the enlightenment conception of the history of philosophy. First, there was the idea of philosophy as the product of the self-conscious and explicit philosophical activity of 'philosophers', rather than as something which, like religion, had sources deep in the wordless experiences of masses of non-intellectuals. Secondly, and involved with this, there was a certain idea of the *form* of philosophical discussion: philosophy consisted of battles between warring schools (or 'sects') each defending some 'system' or '-ism'. (The bulk of the discussion of philosophy's past in the *Encyclopedia* was distributed under headings designating the doctrines of sectarians: 'Aristotelianism', 'Baconism', 'Cartesianism', 'Eclecticism', 'Epicureanism', 'Hobbism', 'Malebranchism', 'Immaterialism', 'Materialists' and 'Spinozist'. The only philosopher to get in under his own name was Locke). The history of philosophy thus became the story of the quarrels with which an inward-looking élite filled their leisure.

The philosophes saw the significance of this image of philosophy much more clearly than did Brucker. They took the apparent separateness of philosophy and ordinary ideas as a reason for denigrating or ridiculing philosophy. If the activities of past philosophers were just the squabbles of an isolated social group then, they thought, their doctrines must simply be the effect of an irresponsible dogmatic sectarianism—'the foolishness of a large number of learned men', as d'Alembert put it[20]. The history of philosophy was told as a story of fools or frauds. Hume, for example, said that:

> Whatever has the air of paradox, and is contrary to the first and most unprejudic'd notions of mankind is often greedily embraced by philosophers, as showing the superiority of their science, which could discover opinions so remote from vulgar conception[21].

Adam Smith drew the conclusion that systems of philosophy were matters of taste and that people could not 'reasonably be much interested about them'[22]; and in general the philosophes decided that traditional philosophy ought to be abandoned, and that the natural reason of non-philosophical minds should take its place. Philosophy had been a battlefield ravaged by the warring schools, and it was time to give up its aggressive dogmatism, and to adopt an attitude of open-minded eclecticism instead.

In his article on History in the *Encyclopedia*, Voltaire described the history of thought as 'little but the account of human errors'; but he believed that historical study of politics, and of everything else, was worthwhile because it threw up instructive examples—or rather warnings. 'The great mistakes of the past', he wrote,

> are extremely useful in every field. The crimes and miseries caused by absurd quarrels cannot be reviewed too often. There can be no doubt that by keeping these quarrels fresh in one's memory, one prevents them from being reborn[23].

Diderot made similar observations in the *Encyclopedia* article 'Eclecticism'—which was largely cribbed from Brucker.

Eclecticism was the opposite of dogmatism or sectarianism. The eclectic, Diderot wrote,

> is a man who, trampling underfoot prejudice, tradition, antiquity, universal opinion, and authority—in a word, everything which enslaves most minds—has the courage to think for himself...The sectarian is a man who has embraced the doctrine of a philosopher; the eclectic, on the other hand, acknowledges no master[24].

As far as the philosophes were concerned, then, philosophy was self-contained, and wholly produced by intellectuals; and the history of philosophy, at least since the decline of Rome, was a story of attitudinising and posturing, captured by a mixture of academic and military metaphor. Philosophy consisted of grandiose and pointless manoeuvres by Warring Schools of Great Philosophers. Great Philosophers wore the uniforms of their schools, and there had never been a philosophical point so well established that they had not fought over it, or a position so absurd that one of them had not tried to defend it. Accounts of the opinions of Great Philosophers of the past became more and more like cautionary tales for the instruction of the young.

Kant and the Modern Academic Tradition
Although Brucker's work was used by the philosophes, he himself was not really one of them. He belonged rather to the modern academic tradition—the tradition of an intelligentsia predominantly engaged in the work of academic institutions. The tradition began in the bourgeois Protestant universities of eighteenth-century Germany which were created to give a liberal education to students who would become politicians, civil servants, or businessmen, rather than scholars, gentlemen or clergy. It was in one of these universities, Jena, that Brucker received his education, and he showed his high opinion of them by including the name of Christian Thomasius, one of the first professors at the university of Halle, in his list of the great 'general philosophers' of the modern age, alongside Hobbes, Bacon, Leibniz and Descartes. Thomasius' achievement, according to Brucker, was that he 'threw off the Sectarian yoke, and introduced eclectic freedom into the German Schools'[25].

The modern academic tradition is concerned with, on the one hand, inducting students into academic subjects by means of textbooks and lectures, and, on the other, with advancing the subjects by means of scholarly works aimed at academics. Brucker answered both these needs. His enormous *History* provided a well-organised inventory of philosophical problems and a definition of the territory with which philosophy was concerned. He also produced a one-volume abridgement[26], specifically adapted to the requirements of students, giving simple classifications of philosophers into their various warring schools. His work continued to be used throughout the nineteenth century.[27]

Within the modern academic tradition it became normal to allot a smaller territory to philosophy than Brucker had done. For example, in his extremely influential and comprehensive series of text books, Christian Wolff, a pupil and later a colleague of Christian Thomasius at Halle, carefully distinguished philosophy from emprical studies and claimed that philosophy comprised only Speculative Philosophy (Logic and Metaphysics), Practical Philosophy (including law and politics) and Aesthetics or the theory of taste. This relatively circumscribed idea of philosophy in its turn reinforced the conviction that the history of philosophy was the history of the self-conscious work of philosophers, and that this developed independently of the ideas of everyone else.

One inheritor of the traditions of the German Protestant universities was Kant, professor of Logic and Metaphysics at the University of Konigsberg. Kant claimed that he had no interest in the history of philosophy, saying that in constructing his own philosophy he would regard 'all that has been done as though undone', and that he would seek intellectual refreshment not from the writings of dead philosophers but from the 'fountain of reason' instead[28]. This does not mean, however, that Kant had no sense of history. In rejecting the past, Kant (like Bacon, Descartes and Pascal) was affirming a definite view of the history of philosophy, and of his place in it. Kant had a more sophisticated view of philosophical progress than most of his predecessors. Like them, he saw philosophy's past in terms of battles between schools of philosophers; but he discerned in it an overall pattern of development which transcended the sectarianism of individual thinkers. Past philosophers had unwittingly participated in a lengthy, oscillating, developing argument, or 'dialectic'—in which the last word was Kant's 'critical philosophy'[29]. Kant thought he had found a safe path between the entrenched positions of the warlike sectarian philosophers of the past. 'At last', he said,

> we have something definite on which to depend in all metaphysical enterprises, which have hitherto, boldly enough but always blindly, attempted everything without discrimination[30].

However, Kant's vision of a progressive, dialectical development in philosophy, which separated him from his enlightenment predecessors, was suppressed in the 'Kantianism' of most of his followers. One of the first works which tried to popularise Kantianism was a *Comparative History of Philosophical Systems*[31] by Joseph-Marie Gerando. This well-organised and elegantly written book came out in Paris in 1804. It aimed to be an 'inductive or comparative history' and to provide a 'natural method for classification', on Baconian principles, applicable to all philosophical 'systems' up to and including Kant's. Gerando set out to identify the basic questions of philosophy and then to classify philosophers into warring schools according to how they had answered them:

> ...If there is a small number of principal questions which, being at the basis of all others, must exercise a natural influence over them...and if, say I, these fundamental questions can be identified, enumerated and clearly defined, one would have a simple and reliable way of indicating, in general terms, the main features, or the essential characteristics, of each doctrine[32].

Gerando thought that the principal questions had been identified as such by Kant, who had tried to synthesise the opposing doctrines involved. But he eliminated Kant's idea of dialectical progress, and even took the view that Kant had failed to provide satisfactory answers to the questions he had identified, and that no one succeeded better than Bacon[33].

Gerando's history was followed by many others, all sharing the same Kantian framework.[34] These Kantian histories projected into the past the idea of philosophy as an autonomous subject, restricted in range and rigorously distinguished from empirical inquiries—rather as the nationalist social and political histories of the next generation described the past terms of national identities; and they enshrined the idea that past philosophers, in constructing their rival 'systems', had been constantly disagreeing concerning a repertoire of Kantian questions.[35] Kant, a 'second Socrates'[36], had made a 'Copernican revolution', showing how philosophy had become a science and an autonomous academic subject.

System and Dialectic in Hegel

Unlike the proponents of Kantianism, Hegel took over Kant's view of dialectical progress in philosophy, in that he believed that the philosophical disagreements of the past had created the possibility of their own resolution and reconciliation. His *Science of Logic* was intended to summarise the result of this process; and the History of Philosophy, for him, was the story of how the elements of this system had been uncovered by the philosophers of the past. But philosophy, for Hegel, was more than an academic subject; the history of philsophy was the story of the progressive realisation of the Idea, of God, or of Spirit, as registered by Reason. (The history of religion was its progress as registered by imagination). In this sense the history of philosophy was the essence of history. And from this point of view any attempt to tell the history of philosophy in terms of sectarian battles about unchanging questions could be seen to be absurd.

> The whole history of philosophy becomes a battlefield covered with the bones of the dead; it is a kingdom formed not merely of dead and lifeless individuals, but of refuted and spiritually dead systems....[37] The stages in the evolution of the Idea there (i.e. in the history of philosophy) seem to follow each other by accident....But it is not so. For these thousands of years the same Architect had directed the work: and that Architect is the one living spirit whose nature is to think and bring to self consciousness what it is....The different systems which the history of philosophy presents are therefore not irreconcilable with unity. We may either say that it is one philosophy at different degrees of maturity; or that the particular principle, which is the groundwork of each system, is but a branch of one

and the same universe of thought. In philosophy the latest birth
of time is the result of all the systems that have preceded it, and
must include their principles; and so, if on other grounds, it
deserves the title of philosophy, it will be the fullest, most
comprehensive, and most adequate system of all.[38]

This vision of the development of philosophy as the discovery
of the science of logic, and as the unfolding of the Idea in
history, implied two insights into the inadequacies of the
stories of warring schools of philosophers which were told in
Enlightenment and Kantian histories of philosophy.

The first fault that Hegel saw in the traditional histories of
philosophy was their assumption that it is possible to define a
set of eternally available theoretical positions and to tell the
history of philosophy by saying which philosophers opted for
which ones. This presupposed that philosophical discussions
arise because different philosophers, having identified the
timeless questions of philosophy in neutral and agreed terms,
answer them in opposite ways. But this attributed an illusory
independence to definitions of possible philosophical
positions, failing to see that any such definition expresses a
particular philosophical outlook, and therefore is not so much
an impartial spectator standing outside the development of
philosophy as a result of the development. At the same time
they proposed an inappropriately mechanical view of
philosophical controversy, in that they assumed that if two
philosophical positions or systems differed they must be
opposed, and that opposed systems could not have anything in
common with one another. Hegel explained an alternative
conception of the relation between different philosophical
systems in the following words:

> The relation...of the earlier to the later systems of philosophy is
> much like the relation of the corresponding stages of the logical
> Idea: in other words, the earlier are preserved in the later, but
> subordinated and submerged. This is the true meaning of a
> much misunderstood phenomenon in the history of
> philosophy—the refutation of one system of philosophy by
> another, of an earlier by a later. Most commonly the refutation
> is taken in a purely negative sense to mean that the system
> refuted has ceased to count for anything, has been set aside
> and done for. Were it so, the history of philosophy would be of

all studies the most saddening, displaying, as it does, the refutation of every system which time has brought forth. Now although it may be admitted that every philosophy has been refuted, it must be in an equal degree maintained, that no philosophy has been refuted, nay, or can be refuted....The refutation of a philosophy, therefore, only means that its barriers are crossed, and its special principle reduced to a factor in the completer principle that follows.[39]

In other words, the historiography of philosophy required a new way of classifying philosophical systems and representing the relations between them. It was necessary to think of opposed systems of philosophy as interpenetrating, so that one system showed its superiority over another not by flatly contradicting it (even if that was what it tried to do) but by incorporating it, or be being *a critique.*

The traditional conception of the relations between philosophical systems had led to anti-philosophical scepticism. The histories of philosophy presented an array of bizarre systems or '-isms' so diverse that it seemed ludicrous to claim that one was superior to another.[40] Hegel's idea that the relations between philosophical systems are dialectical managed to avoid the sceptical conclusion. First, one system might handle its own problems better than another. Secondly, one system might be able to depict another system, together with its problems, explain how it arose, and incorporate it; but not vice-versa; and this would prove its superiority. So Hegel, while doing justice to the difficulty of comparing philosophical systems, allowed for rational choice between them.

Hegel's second insight into the inadequacy of conventional histories of philosophy was concerned with the idea that philosophy is the product of the self-conscious activity of philosophers. Hegel's description of the whole history of philosophy as the work of 'the divine Architect' implies that the development of philosophy is more than the succession of the doctrines of individuals. Indeed it suggests the possibility of a history of philosophy which would not mention individual philosophers at all—and Hegel attempted such a history in the *Phenomenology of Spirit.* For Hegel, the doctrines of philosophers are the highest intellectual expressions of the spirit of their age; this spirit is also manifested in all other human activities and cannot be understood independently of them. Philosophical systems are like waves breaking on beaches, an effect of distant pressures and turbulences; and to tell the story of philosophy in terms of the opinions of the great philosophers would be to write about effects cut off from their causes.[41] The history of philosophy had to be part of spiritual or cultural history in general. (See Chapter Three).

Dialectic and Discontinuity in Marx

Hegel's view of the history of philosophy was an important element in the development of Marx's thought; in fact, Marx's development might be represented as a succession of transformations of Hegel's view of the history of philosophy. Marx wrote his doctoral dissertation (1840-41) on a topic in the history of ancient Greek philosophy, and planned to expand it into a discussion of 'the whole of Greek speculation'. In the Preface he said that Hegel had 'created the history of philosophy as a discipline'.[42] His early Hegelianism about the history of philosophy is expressed in an article of 1842 where he said that 'every true philosophy is the intellectual quintessence of its time' and claimed that 'the same spirit that constructs railways with the hands of workers, constructs philosophical systems in the brains of philosophers'.[43]

Soon afterwards, however, Marx distanced himself from this conception of philosophy and claimed that it gave a false 'semblance of independence' to philosophy[44]. His concept of production, embracing not only material production but also the production of social relations in general, and of religion, art, philosophy, and so on, enabled him to conceive the development of philosophy as determined by causes which lie outside thought altogether. Philosophy did not have a continuous self-contained history stretching back through the centuries, as a sort of indestructible sounding board for some 'essence' of historical development.[45] It was, rather, one of a set of interacting sectors of production, none of which could be understood in complete isolation from the others. Thus Marx was led to depose philosophy from the isolated supremacy given to it by Hegel.

It can be argued that Marx's scepticism about the idea of an essence of historical development distanced him from Hegel's conception of the history of philosophy in another way too; and, in effect, that he abandoned the idea of a dialectical relationship between systems of philosophy. Thus Althusser's Marxism, in keeping with much modern epistemology,[46] searches the development of thought for 'breaks' or 'discontinuities', and pours scorn on the 'continuism' of conventional histories. These discontinuities are supposed to be non-Hegelian and non-dialectical, in the sense of being incapable of co-existing with continuities. And Althusser is doubly anti-Hegelian, for he also asserts that the relation of the mature Marx to Hegel exemplifies this sort of non-dialectical discontinuity.[47]

Althusser's argument must be mistaken. The idea that if one system of thought breaks with another there cannot be any comparison between them is self-defeating. A discontinuity only exists when one system differs from or conflicts with another, and this presupposes that they can be compared. Without continuity there could not be discontinuity, still less theoretical advance.[48] And if Marx had not retained this Hegelian insight, he would have got trapped in the relativism and sceptical despair which Hegel's conception of the dialectical relation between systems had avoided. So although Althusser's dismissal of the idea of continuity between Marxism and other theory is intended to prove the secure scientific status of Marxism, it actually has exactly the opposite effect: it leads to relativism. In order to be able to claim superiority to Classical Political Economy, or to Hegel's political philosophy, or to any other theory, Marx had to adopt Hegel's insight into the possibility of a theory incorporating an opposing theory. And Marx's habit of developing and expounding his theoretical system in the form of critiques of earlier theories was a tribute to it. Marx deliberately and self-consciously placed his theories in the dialectical relationship to past theories which Hegel had seen as the key to the historical development of philosophy.

Academic philosophy and the return to the Enlightenment
In the nineteenth century the production of histories of philosophy became bewilderingly prolific. But the major nineteenth-century histories of philosophy—those of Victor Cousin,[49] which was widely used in English universities, and of

Kuno Fischer,[50] Ueberweg,[51] Renouvier,[52] and Windelband,[53] Ritter[54] and others[55]—paid little attention to the Hegelian criticisms of traditional histories of philosophy, and of course took even less notice of Marxism. The nineteenth-century histories of philosophy were, as a rule, produced by and for academics, who were interested chiefly in self-consciously produced ideas of intellectuals like themselves. Consequently they found most of the Hegelian criticisms of traditional histories of philosophy indigestible. The nineteenth-century histories of philosophy, though mainly Kantian, were essentially a return to enlightenment themes.[56]

Wilhelm Windelband, Professor of Philosophy at the University of Strasbourg, was a typical nineteenth-century historian of philosophy. Writing at the end of the century, he acknowledged Hegel as the creator of the discipline of the history of philosophy, but proceeded to ignore many of Hegel's insights, presenting the development of philosophy as a series of battles between schools of philosophers, culminating in Kant. He was perplexed by what had happened since.

> It is, to be sure, far from true that this apparently final conception of philosophy gained universal acceptance at once. It is rather the case that the great variety of philosophical movements of the nineteenth century has left no earlier form of philosophy unrepeated, and that a luxuriant development of the 'metaphysical need' (Schopenhauer) even brought back, for a time, the inclination to swallow up all human knowledge in philosophy.[57]

The fact that Kant's formulation of a supposedly 'final conception of philosophy' had been followed by a period which 'left no earlier form of philosophy unrepeated' should not really have surprised Windleband. If philosophy's past was filled with warring schools of philosophers occupying opposing 'positions' on timeless questions, the present generation could only reoccupy these positions, or else give up philosophy.

In the nineteenth century, the Kantian names of the doctrines of past philosophers were treated not only as labels applied retrospectively to the past, but also as talismanic formulae which encapsulated all possible doctrines. Opposition between such positions was taken to be the essence of philosophy. But the philosophers' belligerence in defending their chosen positions was often tempered by fatalism: it seemed to most of them that their work could make no difference to anything, since the choice of possible positions would always remain the same.

The pathos of the philosopher's vocation became an important theme of nineteenth-century philosophy. Its meaning was spelt out by the 'neo-Kantian' Charles Renouvier, who was one of the most widely acclaimed French philosophers of his time. Renouvier set out to controvert Hegel's vision of philosophy as an impersonal historical process. For Renouvier, philosophy was essentially personal, and there was no such thing as progress or change in it. Every philosophical doctrine, he claimed, could be reduced to a handful of propositions, which were 'susceptible of being cast in a form in which some of them answer yes, others no, to categorically posed question'.[58] The doctrines themselves had no history. The so-called history of philosophy was really only the story of individuals opting for different philosophical positions; the positions themselves were always there, eternally available and unchanging.

Having devised his classification of philosophical positions, Renouvier was lucid about its implications.

> It is clear that the task of classifying doctrines must result in representing the thinker as being under an obligation to opt between opposing propositions, concerning the principal terms on which the classification is based.[59]

The choice between doctrines, however, had to be left to the individual, and hence 'reason is personal in its determinations'.[60] 'It may well be', Renouvier wrote,

> that doctrinal positions cannot be justified by any method which differs essentially from that followed by the spirit in choosing to adhere to the fundamental articles of a religious faith.[61]

At the end of the nineteenth century Bertrand Russell put forward a similar view of the history of philosophy—although he had rather more faith than Renouvier in the possibility of rational choice between doctrines. Russell stated that 'the philosophies of the past belong to one or other of a few great types—types which in our own day are perpetually recurring'. And in writing about Leibniz he said he would adopt a 'purely philosophical attitude'[62]—'an attitude in which, without regard to dates or influences, we seek simply to discover what are the great types of possible philosophies...'[63]

Since the turn of the century, the outlook of the nineteenth-century historians of philosophy, with their assumption that philosophy had always been a matter of taking sides on eternal issues, has hardly been seriously challenged, and the insights of Hegel, Marx, and Kant, have been ignored.. Even Marxists have generally accepted that bourgeois works on philosophy's past give it the treatment it deserves.[64] The traditional outlook has brought with it the same two alternative conceptions of the tasks of philosophy which haunted both eighteenth and nineteenth century thinkers. The first, 'conservative' conception is that modern philosophers must take up their own positions on the age-old issues defined in the histories of philosophy. (This was the view of the Kantians in the nineteenth century, and has been adopted by thinkers as different as Russell, Lenin, and Althusser in the twentieth). The second, 'revolutionary', conception is that old style philosophy must be abandoned and replaced either by a completely new kind of philosophy or by silence. (This was the view of the philosophes and of Kant in the eighteenth century, and has dominated twentieth century Western philosophy through various rejections of the past, by Wittgenstein and most linguistic philosophy, by the Vienna circle and logical positivism, and by Husserl and phenomenology.) And the choice between these two alternative conceptions has infiltrated twentieth-century philosophy unnoticed, through the vehicle of the histories of philosophy.

Part Two

Histories of Philosophy and the Content of Philosophy: Philosophy as Theory of Knowledge

The battle between Newton and Descartes: Dogmatism, Eclecticism and Scepticism
After its invention in the fourteenth century, the idea of a break between medieval monkish mystification and the clear light of

an heroic new philosophy was constantly revised and brought up to date. By the eighteenth century the turning point had been postponed from the fourteenth century to the first half of the seventeenth. The content of the 'new philosophy' was now identified with the reductive mathematical physical science which had been advocated by Descartes and perfected by Newton. The most important architect of the new philosophy was taken to be Descartes: this is the origin of the cliché which describes Descartes as 'the father of modern philosophy'. But during the eighteenth century Descartes was gradually eclipsed by Newton and Bacon; and as far as the development of physical science was concerned, he lost his reputation as creator of the new style of theories, though he retained some fame as a destroyer of the old.[65]

Despite this changing reputation, Descartes was able to keep his title of 'father of modern philosophy' but only because of changes both in ideas of what philosophy was, and in the interpretation of Descartes' thought. Roughly speaking, philosophy became divorced from physical science and increasingly centred on epistemology or the theory of knowledge. Descartes ceased to be seen as a scientist, and was interpreted as an epistemologist instead. A new account of the origin and nature of modern philosophy crystallised in which the English Channel was regarded as a great philosophical divide with Newton, backed by Bacon, on one side and Descartes on the other.[66] In 1738, for example, Voltaire wrote:

> I see that thinking in France is at a point of great ferment, and that the names of Descartes and Newton seem to be the rallying calls of two parties.[67]

Descartes, or Cartesianism, exemplified the continental vices of dogmatism and high-flown speculation, while the down-to-earth, practical-minded, English thinkers displayed the virtues of eclecticism or non-sectarianism, patiently building up sturdy theories from piecemeal experimentation.[68]

The alleged difference between Cartesians and Newtonians was explained by saying that they held opposite theories of scientific knowledge. It was argued that there were two sources to which knowledge might be traced—a subjective or inner source, comprising the individual's reason or ideas, and an objective or outer source, comprising the facts of sensation or observation. It was said that the Newtonians sought knowledge from the objective source, while Cartesians sought it in the subjective one; that the Newtonians built on a firm basis of real things or facts, while the Cartesians built on a shifting foundation of ideas or theories.

The distinction between the two sources was normally backed up by a comparison—sometimes intended to be taken literally—between knowledge and the nervous system, conceived of as a mechanical network centred on a point in the middle of the head. Newtonianism was then supposed to say that information should be conveyed from the real public world through the sense organs and along the nerves till it reached this centre; and the Cartesian alternative was supposed to be that innate knowledge should be encouraged to grow naturally inside people's heads, with as little disturbance as possible from outside.

There were two popular ways of rounding off this story of international philosophical conflict. One was to say that there were two types of knowledge and that each of the two schools was right about one of them. Thus the naturalist Buffon divided human knowledge into mathematical truths, which depend on human decision, and physical truths, which 'do not depend on us and, instead of being based on suppositions we have made...rest only on facts'. Buffon went on:

> The most delicate and most important point in the study of the sciences is here. To know how to distinguish clearly what is real in a subject from what we have put into it arbitrarily, and to discern clearly the properties that belong to it and those we lend to it, seems to me the foundation of the true method for guiding one's conduct in the sciences.[69]

The alternative dénouement was that all knowledge comes from the senses, in which case the Cartesian school turned out to be wrong not merely about some, but about all types of knowledge—a view favoured by many of the philosophes.[70]

However the story was told, therefore, the Cartesian position was made to seem obviously untenable. It was presented as a stubborn refusal to carry the search for knowledge beyond the confines of one's own head; whereas 'sensible people', as Buffon observed, 'will always recognise that the only and true knowledge is knowledge of facts'.[71] The Cartesians, by definition, were like layabouts, frittering away their inherited wealth, whereas the Newtonians were unafraid to work and earn their living. Descartes was regarded as the father of modern philosophy not because of his scientific work but because he had posed the problem of scepticism. Later philosophers were supposed to have discredited Descartes' 'reply to the sceptic', and to have been 'doing battle' with scepticism ever since. Descartes' engaging, if untrue, story about how he withdrew into lonely meditation and doubted the existence of everything but his own thoughts, his presentation of his cosmological and physiological theories as fables, and his remarks about 'innate ideas' were promoted to a position at the centre of his philosophy, displacing his physics, cosmology and mathematics; and his works were read as defences of the patent folly of trying to gain scientific knowledge without bothering about 'facts'. The Cartesians, according to one Newtonian, 'were like people who took care to keep their eyes scrupulously shut in order that they might reason freely'.[72] Leibniz and his followers were normally distinguished from the Cartesians, but only to be criticised in similar terms.[73]

The idea of a struggle between Cartesians and Newtonians does have some historical foundation. The Newtonians, beginning with Newton himself, detested Descartes for his confidence that all physical phenomena could be explained mechanistically, without reference to divine activity or final causes. They despised Cartesians for being content with non-mathematical generalities, for refusing to believe in the existence of vacuums and for adhering to Descartes' explanation of gravitation in terms of whirling vortices of matter. But the idea that these differences between Cartesians and Newtonians were due to their occupying opposite positions on an extremely abstract question about the sources of knowledge is a myth of eighteenth-century historiography, though it is traceable ultimately to Newton. Descartes had never seen himself as taking up any such position. In fact he would not have thought that scientists could ever be confronted with the choice of starting from 'objective' facts or starting from 'subjective' ideas;[74] and he would have been right.

The 'choice' presupposes that the ideas one employs are a matter of individual caprice, so that it is best not to rely on them in one's investigations, whereas in fact the selection of ideas is not arbitrary or subjective, and one cannot investigate facts without employing ideas. In short, the general question about the source of knowledge which, in the eighteenth century, divided the Newtonians and Cartesians, scarcely makes sense; but this 'question', whether called the 'problem of scepticism', 'the problem of the relation between thought and being', 'epistemology' or by any other name, has dominated conceptions of the history of philosophy ever since.

In the eighteenth century the word 'dogmatism' and the words 'eclecticism' and 'scepticism' were sometimes used to name the alternative answers to the supposed question about the source of knowledge, and Kant used this terminology in explaining his own 'critical philosophy'. He named defenders of the two positions and claimed that he himself had combined them in a philosophy which had the strengths of both and the weaknesses of neither[75]—a formula which has been very popular in philosophy ever since. Soon, however, the terminology of 'dogmatism' and 'scepticism' lost its popularity, and was replaced by the words 'materialism', 'rationalism' and 'empiricism', all defined by reference to the supposed dispute about the source of knowledge. Gerando tried to systematise this vocabulary:

> If we now seek the true point of separation at which the divergence of sects begins, we will find that it always resides in the age old battle between experience and reasoning, between the senses and reflection, between facts and principles, between instinct and speculation, between human ideas and the testimony of nature, or in the need to reconcile these apparently contradictory authorities[76].

Simplifying some distinctions of Kant's[77], Gerando divided the issues in this 'age old battle' into three questions about human knowledge—'the three long battles which devastate the empire of philosophy'[78]. The first question was about the certainty of human knowledge, and it divided philosophers into dogmatists and sceptics; the second was about its origin, and divided them into rationalists and empiricists or experimentalists; and the third, about its reality or objectivity, divided them into materialists and idealists.

Idealism, realism and materialism
The word 'materialism' had not traditionally been used as a name for an attitude to the nature of knowledge. In the seventeenth and eighteenth centuries, the word was used either to refer to the idea that a reductive, mechanistic physical science gives a complete account of the physical world, or to the more extreme idea that it gives a complete account of the whole of reality. In these contexts, materialism was regarded as a typical doctrine of Descartes and Cartesians[79], and also as closely allied with atheism, particularly through the writings of eighteenth-century French thinkers like Holbach and La Mettrie. The opposite of materialism was spiritualism or immaterialism, of which the most extreme protagonist was Berkeley, who had denied that there could be any such thing as the matter which reductive physical theory purported to describe.

The situation became more complicated when the word 'idealism' was added to the discussion. Leibniz used the word to refer to Berkeley's immaterialism[80]; but when later writers called Berkeley an idealist, it was because of his supposed view of knowledge rather than because of his rejection of the concept of matter. Berkeley was an idealist because he thought (they alleged) that the only thing people can know about is their own ideas or what goes on in their own heads. (Thus his reputation came to resemble—amazingly—that of Descartes). It was with Berkeley in mind that Diderot wrote in 1749:

> The word 'idealists' is applied to those philosophers who, having immediate knowledge only of their own existence and of the succession of sensations inside them, do not acknowledge the existence of anything else. It is an extravagant system, which could only have been thought up by blind people, and a system which—to the shame of the human mind—is the most difficult to refute, though the most absurd of all[81].

This new, epistemological sense of 'idealism' meant that Descartes and the Cartesians, as viewed by the Newtonians, had to be taken out of the materialist camp and put with the idealists instead. Kant regarded Berkeley and Descartes as different kinds of idealists[82].

Kant claimed that his critical philosophy had destroyed idealism[83]; but later writers have usually classified Kant as an idealist. Hegel did so for example; but when he spoke of 'the idealism of speculative philosophy' he meant to praise it for being dialectical as opposed to abstract and metaphysical[84]; and for Hegel only idealism deserved the name of philosophy. But Hegel also used the word 'idealism' in the same disparaging way as Diderot had done, as a label for philosophies, like Berkeley's and Hume's, in which 'the idea itself is made the object'[85]. In this context, for Hegel, 'idealism' was the opposite of 'realism', and not of 'materialism', as it had been in Leibniz, Gerando and others.

The idea of philosophy as consisting mainly, or even entirely, of a battle between idealism and materialism has survived in Marxism, beginning with Marx's attempt to explain his relation to Hegel. In *The Holy Family,* he wrote that Hegel's *Phenomenology* was an attempt to teach

> the art of changing real objective chains that exist outside me, into mere ideal, mere subjective chains existing in me, and thus to change all exterior, palpable struggles into struggles of pure thought[86].

There is a similar statement in an Afterword to *Capital I* where Marx tried to distinguish his position from Hegel's by saying: 'the ideal is nothing but the material world reflected in the mind of man and translated into forms of thought'[87].

Engels's *Ludwig Feuerbach* (1886) gives a lucid account of the relationship of Marxism both to eighteenth-century mechanical materialism and to Hegel. But the discussion takes completely for granted the traditional assumptions about the territory of philosophy:

> The great basic question of all philosophy, especially of more recent philosophy, is that concerning the relation of thinking and being . . . The answers which the philosophers gave to this question split them into two great camps. Those who asserted the primacy of spirit to nature . . . comprised the camp of idealism. The others, who regarded nature as primary, belong to the various schools of materialism[88].

The way out of this problem, as Engels stated it, was equally traditional:

> It is no longer a question anywhere of inventing interconnections from out of our brains, but of discovering them in the facts.[89]

These attempts to give a simple definition of Marx's relationship to Hegel, or of Marxism in general, in terms of categories (idealism and materialism) and imagery (the ideas in people's heads and the real world outside) taken from Kantian or pre-Kantian histories of philosophy are obviously very crude; furthermore, they suggest a separation between the world of thought, conceived as completely private, personal and autonomous, and the real historical world, which is foreign to Marxism. Consequently the terms 'idealism' and 'materialism' have not been able to provide Marxist theory with the simple, self-explanatory definitions which they seem to promise. Their meaning is a problem in Marxist theory, rather than an agreed starting point.

Rationalism and Empiricism
The distinction between rationalism and empiricism, though it had been made by Bacon[90] and Leibniz[91], was first systematically developed in the works of the nineteenth-century historians of philosophy, who used it to gesture in the direction of the supposed opposition between Newtonian and Cartesian approaches to science. However, it took some time for historians to decide which philosophers belonged with the Newtonian empiricists, and which with the Cartesian rationalists. Kant had called Locke and Aristotle empiricists, but for him the opposite of 'empiricism' was 'no-ologism', a school represented by Plato and Leibniz[92]. Tenneman put Descartes and Leibniz together in the category of rationalists, and Locke, Newton and Hume into that of English experimentalism[93]. Hegel used the words 'empiricism' and 'rationalism' to distinguish two tendencies within what he called 'idealism' in the dismissive sense, but unlike Kant he saw Locke as a rationalist rather than as an empiricist[94]. Locke was not normally called an empiricist until the 1860s[95]. Some time later it became accepted that Locke, Berkeley and Hume were

the main empiricists, and Descartes, Spinoza and Leibniz the main rationalists[96], and this basic membership of the two schools has been taken for granted ever since. In 1912, for instance, Russell wrote:

> The empiricists—who are best represented by the British philosophers, Locke, Berkeley and Hume—maintained that all our knowledge is derived from experience; the rationalists— who are represented by the continental philosophers of the seventeenth century, especially Descartes and Leibniz— maintained that, in addition to what we know by experience, there are certain 'innate ideas' and 'innate principles', which we know independently of experience[97].

Russell went on to say that 'It has now become possible to decide with some confidence as to the truth or falsehood of these opposing schools'[98], and came down, rather surprisingly, on the side of the rationalists; though later he was to come down with equal confidence on the other side[99]. The best way of avoiding such vacillations is, of course, to put the concepts of empiricism and rationalism back into their Kantian context and to say that the two schools were dissolved and merged by Kant. This is what C. R. Morris did in 1931:

> It is well known that in the seventeenth century there began a great era in modern philosophy. It was inevitable that men should begin the attempt to square their beliefs about God and the universe with the new theories of science. This attempt branched along two main lines; and there arose the great school of rationalism on the Continent of Europe, and that of Empiricism in Britain. On the whole it seems to be the agreed verdict of the history of philosophy that both lines of thought were in themselves abortive. Both were gathered up in the philosophy of Kant.

The concepts of empiricism and rationalism have been one of the unquestioned heirlooms of philosophy ever since.

Philosophy and the theory of knowledge
Modern philosophers often identify the theoretical options open to them by reference to the positions of the old warring schools—materialism,   idealism,   realism,   scepticism, rationalism or empiricism; and the mythic image of Descartes

is still often invoked as a warning of the fate which awaits over-ambitious theoretical speculators. And along with these echoes of traditional histories of philosophy there comes the theory that the great philosophers, at least since Descartes, have been preoccupied with 'doing battle with the sceptic' and trying to prove that it is possible to know about a world beyond one's ideas. Thus a certain type of epistemological problem overshadows religious, ethical, political and social or psychological and physical theory, and thereby crowds out or distorts many of the main concerns of the thinkers enlisted as philosophers by the History of Philosophy. A dubious eighteenth-century view of the content of Philosophy insinuates itself into modern ideas disguised as an innocent classification of the Great Dead Philosophers.

Part Three
History and Philosophy

'Historical approaches' to philosophy
The study of philosophy's past has not appealed much to recent Western philosophers (though it has been rather more popular in continental Europe than in the English-speaking world[101]). There are two main reasons for this. The first is that, accepting the lesson of the histories of philosophy, that past philosophy has consisted of endless, destructive, pointless sectarian battles, they have regarded philosophy's past as an embarrassment, and have wished to pass over it in silence. They have felt that modern philosophers have no more reason for studying past systems of philosophy than radio engineers have for studying smoke signals. Philosophers in the 'analytic' tradition are one example. They have taken over the neo-Kantian idea that nineteenth-century philosophy was almost entirely overgrown with a luxuriant, self-indulgent rhetoric, for which Hegel was largely responsible[102]. But they believe that at about the turn of the century philosophy came of age and that the humiliations and disappointments of its over-ambitious adolescence gave place to a mature and sober understanding of its limitations, allowing it to take up the less glamorous, but more sensible, task of trying to establish a few

incontestable, if unexciting, truths. The writings of past philosophers then appear as the flotsam and jetsam deposited on the beaches of history by retreating tides of incautious speculation. Of course, this can be material to philosophise about, and it may even contain a few things which can be put to use. As R. M. Hare says:

> If old mistakes are resuscitated, it is often impossible to do more than restate, in as clear a way as possible, the old arguments against them. Philosophical mistakes are like dandelions in the garden; however carefully one eradicates them, there are sure to be some more next year, and it is difficult to think of novel ways of getting rid of their familiar faces. 'Naturalistas expellas furca, tamen usque recurrent'. But in fact the best implement is still the old fork invented by Hume.[103]

Such tokens of respect to philosophers of long ago are two-sided, however: they are normally offered on the understanding that most past philosophers were not really very good at the subject, so that those who show glimmerings of promise deserve lavish encouragement.

In spite of this sort of condescension, teachers of philosophy often adopt what they call a 'historical approach' to philosophical problems. Stories of the weary soldier Descartes locking himself in a cottage heated by an old-fashioned stove and musing about the uncertainties which beset man's quest for knowledge, seem to get students into a receptive mood so that philosophical ideas can be slipped into their minds relatively easily. (It was, after all, for similar reasons that Descartes made up these stories in the first place).

This sort of 'historical approach' to philosophy illustrates the second reason for the relative neglect of philosophy's past by modern philosophers. It is that they approach philosophy's past through the concepts provided by the History of Philosophy, with its thoroughly unhistorical conception of 'philosophical positions', and consequently get the impression that studying philosophy's past is a diversion from real philosophical activity. The 'historical approach' offered by the History of Philosophy simply means discussing positions in the chronological order in which they happen to have been occupied by Great Philosophers, and adding a little human interest by sketching something of the lives of the

Philosophers; it does not mean discussing the history of the "positions" themselves.

Philosophical understanding and historical knowledge
The paradoxical thing about the History of Philosophy is that it is deeply anti-historical. If its assumptions were correct, then historical knowledge would be irrelevant to philosophy, and the study of philosophy's past would be a waste of the philosopher's time; there would be a choice between history and reason, between 'historical' and 'philosophical' approaches to philosophy.

This choice was described by Bertrand Russell in the Preface to his book on Leibniz. He distinguished between inquiries into the *'relations* of philosophies' and inquiries into 'the philosophies themselves', saying that if one adopted a 'purely philosophical attitude' one would avoid discussing philosophical doctrines 'psychologically'. Instead,

> Without regard to dates or influences, we seek simply to discover what are the great types of possible philosophies, and guide ourselves in the search by investigating the systems advocated by the great philosophers of the past. . . . By what process of development he came to this opinion, though in itself an important and interesting question, is logically irrelevant to the inquiry how far this opinion itself is correct. . . . Philosophic truth and falsehood, in short, rather than historical fact, are what primarily demands our attention in this inquiry.[104]

Part of Russell's point here is that there is a difference between identifying someone's opinions and discovering whether they are true, and that it is legitimate to concentrate on one rather than the other—which is obviously true. But this does not imply that historical questions are, as Russell puts it, 'logically irrelevant' to philosophical ones.

Russell's book unwittingly betrays the segregation of history and philosophy proposed in its preface. It is true that, as Russell himself said, he 'pruned away' minor inconsistencies in Leibniz's thought in order to make its main features stand out clearly; but this did not mean he was not writing history. It is also true that Russell's book is very misleading as to what Leibniz believed (see Chapter Two); but though this makes it bad history, it does not make it philosophy. Russell's account of Leibniz from a 'purely philosophical' point of view, in fact, turned out to be a (rather inaccurate) historical book in spite of itself.

The attempt to exclude history from philosophy, and philosophy from history, is not so much impractical as theoretically impossible. Ascribing a belief to someone involves making some sense of it by articulating it into one's own language and concepts. Therefore one could not go into what Russell calls the 'important and interesting' question of dates and influences in philosophy's past, or of who thought what and why, without employing philosophical understanding.

Nor can philosophical understanding disconnect itself from historical knowledge.[105] One must identify a philosophical, or any other, opinion, in order to undertake 'the inquiry how far this opinion is correct'; and Russell could not have sustained his disdainful view of historical knowledge if he had not—on philosophical principle rather than out of laziness—ignored the complexities of this process of identification. Identifying a belief involves locating it in the system of beliefs, some of which may be unconscious; and in the end it involves placing them in a context of things other than beliefs. It requires knowledge about the language in which they were expressed, about the communicative practices in which they were inserted, and about the conceptions of intellectual boundaries[106] and of the current state of the argument which underlie their expression, and so on.

Members of an inward-looking intellectual community, of course, may understand one another well enough without conscious use of such historical knowledge. They may be as unaware of it as of the air they breathe. But they need only try communicating with outsiders to realise that they depend on it implicitly. Even an isolated individual who only wanted to work out his own ideas for himself would need such historical knowledge: identifying one's own ideas involves most of the same problems as identifying other people's. After all, one does not create 'one's own' ideas for oneself, or out of nothing. There is therefore no such thing as a really non-historical approach to philosophical ideas[107], or a philosophical outlook which does not involve a conception of history—and especially of the history of philosophy.

Conclusion: The Ideological Function of the History of Philosophy

The historical consciousness of modern philosophy is the orthodox History of Philosophy, which has been passed from generation to generation, from professor to student, with up-datings and minor revisions, from the eighteenth century to the present. In Part One I suggested that in spite of the insights of Marx, Hegel and to some extent Kant, it has perpetuated the misleading Enlightenment idea of philosophy as consisting of battles between warring schools of philosophers; and in Part Two, I have argued that it systematically distorts the ideas of its Great Philosophers by presenting them as primarily a response to epistemological questions. Finally, in Part Three, I have argued that all philosophical understanding must involve some conception of history, whereas the orthodox History of Philosophy, instead of improving and extending such conceptions, ignores or despises them. If I am right, then the orthodox History of Philosophy is a fabric of illusions and distortions.

There is, however, a possible defence for some aspects of the History of Philosophy. Provided one can specify the concepts and principles which constitute philosophy—as Hegel, for example, tried to do in his *Science of Logic*[108]—one can then record various past insights into it and call this a history of philosophy. This, after all, is how the histories of the sciences are normally written, and it could be described as the implicit methodology of the History of Philosophy.

However, there are difficulties in this defence. First, philosophy as we know it encompasses almost any kind of abstract, conceptual puzzlement or consternation that people may happen to feel and this makes it impossibly difficult to provide any definition of the 'principles of philosophy'—though such a definition might be provided for mathematical logic and linguistics, which are arguably parts of philosophy. Secondly, a record of past insights in philosophy would scarcely deserve the name 'history of philosophy', since it would not explain the real historical development of philosophy. At best, such a record would be a deliberately biased history, recounting the victories, but not the defeats; or a bowdlerised history, missing out the more unseemly or picaresque events of philosophy's past. To call such an account a history would be like confusing descriptions of exquisite flowers with scientific explanations of their growth.

The History of Philosophy is perhaps less important for what it says than for what it conceals. It hides the way in which philosophical problems and the range of conceivable philosophical 'positions' vary historically; and the ways in which the present—including one's own philosophical outlook—is a product of the past. Nor does it address itself to the problem of how human conceptual resources have expanded and developed in the course of history or how they can become material forces; still less does it try to locate the activities of intellectuals or 'philosophers' in these developments. This enables it to present philosophy as a self-contained, eternal sector of intellectual production, where battles between professionals have been fought since the beginning of time. No one accepts responsibility for this curious offspring of bad historiography and bad philosophy; but in the unconscious depths of academic and intellectual life, the History of Philosophy is as active as ever. Constantly reproducing a crazy picture of philosophy as a sort of unhistorical disembodied spirit, with a history of its own going back like a tunnel through the centuries, it is one of our most powerful intellectual myths.

Notes

1   See Karl Korsch, 'Marxism and Philosophy' (1923) in *Marxism and Philosophy,* trans. Halliday, London, New Left Books, 1970, esp. pp 34-38.

2   But see John Passmore (ed.), *The historiography of the history of philosophy, History and Theory,* Beiheft 5, (1965) especially Passmore's article; and *La Filosofia della Storia della Filosofia,* Milan and Rome, 1954, especially Martial Gueroult's article, and *The History of Philosophy as a Philosophical Problem,* a special issue of *The Monist,* Vol 53/No 4, October 1969.

3   Medieval Christianity had been understandably hostile to the study of the history of thought, simply because it clearly revealed

that the best thinkers were Pagans, not Christians. See Peter Gay, *The Enlightenment* (two volumes), London, Weidenfeld, 1967, 1971, Vol I, pp 218-220.

4 See Erwin Panofsky, *Renaissance and Renascences in Western Art*, 2nd edn., 1965, pp 108-113.

5 But the study of both ancient and medieval philosophical texts, if not the history of philosophy as a whole, was maintained in certain universities e.g. Leipzig, where Jakob Thomasius introduced his pupil Leibniz to them.

6 'Plato says one thing, Aristotle another, Epicurus another; Telesio, Campanella, Bruno, Basson, Vanini—all the innovators—they all say something different'. Letter to Beeckmann, 17 x 30.

7 Cf. *De Augmentis*, II iv; III i.

8 Baillet, *Vie de M. Descartes*, 1691, Vol II, p 531. Similar remarks were made by Bacon and Pascal; see *Novum Organon*, 184; Pascal, *Pensees*, II 271.

9 G. H. Lewes described Stanley's *History* as 'the delight of my boyhood—a great work, considering the era in which it was produced'. (*Biographical History of Philosophy*, 1846, Preface).

10 Georg Horn (Hornius), *Historiae Philosophicae Libri Septem, quibus de origine, successione, sectis et vita philosophorum ab orbe condito ad nostram aetatem agitur*, Leyden, 1655.

11 This theory is due to St Augustine (*City of God*, VIII ix).

12 Bréhier describes it as 'the first general history of philosophy' (*History of Philosophy*, Vol I, trans. Joseph Thomas, Chicago University Press, 1963, p 12).

13 *Historia Critica Philosophiae a mundi incunabulis ad nostram aetatem agitur* (5 vols., 1742-1744). Brucker's work was continued in Dietrich Tiedemann's *Geist der Speculativen Philosophie*, 7 vols., Marburg 1791-97.

14 Brucker, 1767 edn., in six volumes, vol IV, p 3, trans. William Enfield, London 1791, Vol II, p 399.

15 See John Lough, *The Encyclopédie*, London, Longman, 1971, p 146; see also Gay, *The Enlightenment*, Vol I, pp 346-8.

16 There were some attempts to represent the middle ages as an advance on antiquity, in order to display history as the steady progress of human reason, but these were exceptions. Turgot, for instance, in an undatable fragment, proposed the theory that thought had developed from a theological form, through a metaphysical form, until finally it reached a positive form—a scheme to be adapted by August Comte a century later. See Gay, II, p 109, n 6. See also Condorcet's *Esquisse d'une Histoire des Progrès de l'Esprit de l'Esprit Humain*, 1793. In addition, André

Deslandes had protested against the treatment of the history of philosophy as a history of sects in his *Histoire Critique de la Philosophie*, Amsterdam, 1739.

[17] See Gay, Vol I, pp 209, 227, 36, 226.

[18] *Encyclopédie*, VIII, p 223; see also d'Alembert's article *Ecole* and Diderot's *Expérimental*.

[19] Cf. Bréhier, op. cit., p 17.

[20] A remark appended by d'Alembert to the article *Cabale*. See R. Grimsley, *Jean d'Alembert*, OUP, 1963, p 18.

[21] *Treatise of Human Nature*, 1739-40, I, ii, 1.

[22] *The Theory of Moral Sentiments*, Part I, Section I, Ch IV; in Selby-Bigge (ed.), *British Moralists*, 1897, Vol I, p 274.

[23] *Encyclopedia* VIII, pp 220-223.

[24] *Ibid*. V, p 270.

[25] Brucker, trans. Enfield, Vol II, p 566.

[26] *Institutiones Historiae Philosophicae Usui Academicae Juventutes Adornatae*, 1747.

[27] An English abridgement by William Enfield came out in 1791. In an *Encyclopaedia Britannica* article, Sir William Hamilton of Edinburgh University said Brucker's history was 'still the best', and at the end of the century T.S. Bain of St. Andrews referred to it as 'standard work'. The French translation and abridgement was done by Victor Cousin in 1829. However, Brucker's History was not always highly regarded. Hegel called it 'useless ballast' (*Vorlesungen über die Geschichte der Philosophie*, 3 vols., Berlin, 1833-6; trans. Haldane; *History of Philosophy*, three vols., Routledge, 1892, Vol I, p 112); and G. H. Lewes remarked 'Dr Enfield's abridgement possesses all the faults of arrangement and dullness of Brucker's work, to which he has added no inconsiderable dullness and blundering of his own'; and commented that though 'extensively bought, it certainly has not been extensively read'. (*Biographical History of Philosophy*, preface).

[28] *Prolegomena to Any Future Metaphysics*, 1783, Introduction. See also Sergio Givone, *La Storia della Filosofia secondo Kant*, Milan 1972.

[29] According to Kant, this dialectic had the following form: the first step was dogmatic, the second, in reaction against the first, was sceptical, and the third was critical (*Critique of Pure Reason*, trans. Kemp Smith, p 607).

[30] *Prolegomena*, para. 31.

[31] *Histoire Comparée des Systèmes de Philosophie*, 3 vols., Paris, 1804.

[32] Gerando, Vol I, pp xii-xiii.

33 *Ibid.* Vol II, p 181.
34 The first of these was Gottfried Wilhelm Tenneman, who himself
    translated Gerando's work into German. Tenneman published
    instalments of his own project on the history of philosophy
    (*Geschichte der Philosophie,* 11 vols., Leipzig, 1798-1819) over a
    period of twenty years, but never completed it. In 1812, however,
    he produced a one volume abridgement for students (*Grundriss
    der Geschichte der Philosophie für den akademischen
    Unterricht*). This abridgement was widely used both in the
    original and in French and English translations. The French
    translation was done by Victor Cousin (*Manuel de l'Histoire de
    la Philosophie,* 2 vols., Paris, 1830). The English translation, by
    Rev. Arthur Johnson, was the *Manual of the History of
    Philosophy,* Oxford, 1832).
35 'The philosophical sciences stood in need of more accurate
    limitations and more completely scientific forms'—Tenneman,
    Grundriss, trans. Johnson, p 399.
36 *Ibid.* p 403.
37 *History of Philosophy,* Vol I, p 17.
38 *Logic* (*Encyclopedia*), 1817, Ch. 1, para. 13, trans. Wallace,
    OUP, p 22.
39 *Ibid.* para. 83, pp 159-160; see also the first part of Hegel's
    'Preface' to *The Phenomenology of Spirit.*
40 Cf. the concept of paradigms in T. S. Kuhn's *The Structure of
    Scientific Revolutions,* Chicago UP, 1962.
41 'It is thus *One Individuality* which, presented in its essence as
    God, is honoured and enjoyed in *Religion*; which is exhibited as
    an object of sensuous contemplation in *Art*; and is apprehended
    as an intellectual conception in *Philosophy*'. Hegel, *Philosophy
    of History,* trans. Sibree (New York, Dover, 1956, p 53, cf. p 49).
42 See Karl Marx and Frederick Engels, *Collected Works,* Vol I,
    Moscow, 1975, pp 29-30.
43 *Collected Works,* Vol I, p 195.
44 'In direct contrast to German philosophy which descends from
    heaven to earth, here we ascend from earth to heaven . . .
    Morality, religion, metaphysics, all the rest of ideology and their
    corresponding forms of consciousness, thus no longer retain
    their semblance of independence. They have no history, no
    development. . .' Marx and Engels, *The German Ideology,* 1846,
    Part One (Ed. C. J. Arthur, London, 1970), p 47.
45 For a critique of Hegel's concept of history as the 'expression' of
    an essence, see 'Contradiction and Overdetermination' in Louis
    Althusser, *for Marx,* trans. Brewster, Penguin, 1969,
    and also his 'Marxism is not a Historicism', *Reading Capital,*

trans. Brewster, NLB, 1970, p 119. The same target is attacked in E. H. Gombrich, *In Search of Cultural History,* OUP, 1969.

[46] See, for example, the work of Bachelard, Canguilhem, and Foucault. See also M. Fichant and M. Pecheux, *Sur l'histoire des Sciences,* Paris, Maspero, 1971.

[47] For Althusser's application of the concept of 'break' to Marx, see his *Réponse à John Lewis,* Paris, Maspero, 1973, pp 51-63.

[48] To use an Althusserian example, the danger of speaking uncritically about the 'break' is that it might make one incapable of explaining how the relation between Marxism and, say, classical physics, differs from that between Marxism and classical political economy.

[49] *Cours de Philosophie,* Paris, 1828. Cousin's history was based on the idea of reconciling the two great schools of idealism and sensualism, in a synthetic eclecticism.

[50] *Geschichte der neuern Philosophie,* (8 vols.), Mannheim and Heidelberg, 1855-93.

[51] *Grundriss der Geschichte der Philosophie,* Berlin, 1863.

[52] *Esquisse d'une Classification Systématique des Doctrines Philosophiques,* 2 vols., Paris, 1885-6.

[53] *Geschichte der Philosophie,* Freiburg, 1892.

[54] Ritter's history (*Geschichte der Philosophie,* 12 vols., Hamburg 1829-53) culminates with Kant and was widely used in France and England (see the Introduction to Lewes's *Biographical History*).

[55] For example, those of Rheinhold (1828-30) and Erdmann (1866).

[56] The main exception to this generalisation is the work of Comte. His ideas were taken up in England by J. S. Mill and by G. H. Lewes, who presented Comte's positivism as the culmination of the history of philosophy in his *Biographical History of Philosophy,* London, 1846.

[57] *History of Philosophy,* trans. Tufts, Macmillan, 1893, p 4.

[58] *Esquisse,* Vol I, p 3.

[59] *Ibid.* Vol II, p 28.

[60] *Ibid.* Vol II, p 355, n 1.

[61] 'Esquisse d'une Classification systematique des doctrines philosophiques, *La Critique Religieuse,* V, July 1822, p 183; cited in E. Bréhier, 'La notion de Renaissance dans l'Histoire de la Philosophie' (originally OUP 1933), reprinted in Bréhier's *Etudes de Philosophie Moderne,* Paris, PUF, 1965.

[62] *A Critical Exposition of the Philosophy of Leibniz,* London, Unwin, 1900, pp xi-xii.

[63] One exception is the work of Catholic philosophers in France, who in an attempt to create a modern Christian philosophy have tried to overturn the periodisation which separates the middle from the modern age. See e.g. Gilson's *Etudes sur le Rôle de la Pensée Médiévale dans la Formation du Système Cartésien*, Paris, Vrin, 1930.

[64] 'Lenin and Philosophy' in *Lenin and Philosophy and other Essays*, trans. Brewster, NLB, 1971, and *Réponse à John Lewis* contain Althusser's definition of philosophy as class struggle in theory, and their corollary that 'A la limite, les thèses philosophiques sont "sans age" '. (*Réponse*, p 61). The classic Marxist treatment of the history of philosophy is Engels's *Ludwig Feuerbach and the end of classical German philosophy* (1866), in Marx and Engels, *Selected Works* (Moscow 1962), 2 vols., Vol II, pp 358-402, which argues that Hegel summed up and brought to an end the history of philosophy (p 365). See further below pp 24-5.

[65] See Jonathan Rée, *Descartes*, Allen Lane, London, 1974, pp 151-7.

[66] This version of events was encouraged by a rather nationalist Royal Society in England. As early as 1715 Leibniz made the Hanovarian succession to the English throne the occasion for offering his services as an international intellectual mediator—even though, as far as the Royal Society was concerned, Leibniz was himself a chief villain, because he disputed Newton's claim to have invented the infinitesimal calculus. See the letters of Leibniz, Conti and Caroline, Princess of Wales in A Robinet (ed.), *Correspondance Leibniz-Clarke*, Paris, PUF, 1957, pp 13-22.

[67] Letter to Maupertuis, 1738. Quoted in A. Vartanian, *Diderot and Descartes*, Princeton Univeristy Press, 1953, p 138; see also Voltaire's *Lettres Philosophiques*.

[68] An influential exposition of this point was contained in Condillac's *Traité des Systèmes* (1749). Cf. Vartanian, *op. cit.*, p 167. Brucker states that Descartes was the founder of a sect, although he himself was an eclectic (1767 edition, Vol I, pp 39-45).

[69] Buffon, *Oeuvres Philosophiques*, ed. Pineteau, p 26. See Gay, *The Enlightenment*, Vol II, P 154.

[70] See, for example, d'Alembert's *Discours Préliminaire* to the *Encyclopédie* (1971) Part One. See also Diderot's *Pensées sur l'Interprétation de la Nature*.

[71] *Oeuvres*, (ed. Pineteau) p 15; Gay, Vol II, p 153.

72   Pluche, *Histoire du Ciel,* (2 vols., Paris, 1739) II 221, quoted in Vartanian, *op. cit.* p 195.

73   See Gerando, *op. cit.*, Vol I, p 27; and Condillac's *Traite des Systèmes.*

74   On one occasion when Descartes did accept, at least provisionally, the distinction between two possible sources of knowledge, he used the imagery which later became normal in order to place himself on the side which he was later thought to have opposed, expressing contempt for 'those philosophers who, ignoring experience, expect truth to spring from their brains like Minerva from the head of Zeus' *Rules for the Direction of the Mind,* V; *Oeuvres,* Ed. Adam and Tannery, Vol X, p 380.

75   *Critique of Pure Reason,* p 666; 'The History of Pure Reason'. See also Hegel, *Logic (Encyclopedia),* para. 32.

76   Gerando, *Histoire Comparée,* Vol I, p 24.

77   *Critique of Pure Reason,* pp 667-8.

78   Gerando, *op. cit.,* Vol II, p 181.

79   See for example Cudworth's *True Intellectual System of the Universe* (1678). Also Eucken, *Geschichte der Philosophischen Terminologie* (1879), reprinted Olms, Hildesheim, 1964, p 94.

80   For Leibniz the main representatives of idealism and materialism were Plato and Epicurus respectively. Materialism had its modern representatives in extreme Cartesians. Leibniz conceived it to be his task to reconcile the two sides. See *Réponse aux Réflections de Bayle, Philosophische Schriften,* Ed. Gerhardt, Vol IV, pp 554, 559-60.

81   *Lettre sur les Aveugles* (1749), *Oeuvres Philosophiques,* Ed. Vernière, Garnier, Paris, 1964, p 114.

82   *Critique of Pure Reason,* p 224, *Prolegomena to Any Future Metaphysics,* Appendix. For Wolff's use of the word as part of a systematic classification, see Eucken, *op. cit.,* p 132n.

83   e.g. *Critique of Pure Reason,* p 17 (Preface to Second Edition).

84   *Logic,* Para. 32, p 67.

85   *History of Philosophy,* Vol III, p 163.

86   *The Holy Family,* Moscow, 1956, p 111.

87   *Capital I,* Penguin, 1976, p 192.

88   *Ludwig Feuerbach,* MESW, Vol II, pp 369-70.

89   *Ibid.* p 400. Cf. 'Socialism, Utopian and Scientific' (1880): 'Hegel was an idealist. To him the thoughts within his brain were not the more or less abstract pictures of actual things and processes, but, conversely, things and their evolution were only the realised pictures of the "Idea'. . .' (*Selected Works,* Vol II, p 133).

90   'The empiricists', said Bacon, 'are like ants, who simply heap things up and consume them. The rationalists, on the other hand,

spin webs out of themselves like spiders. The best method,
however, is that of the bee, who selects material from the flowers
of both the gardens and the fields, and at the same time
transforms and digests it by his own powers' (*Redargutio
Philosophorum, Works*, Ed. Ellis and Spedding, Vol III, p 583).
91   Cf. Eucken, *op. cit.* p 105, n 3.
92   *Critique of Pure Reason*, p 666; 'The History of Pure Reason'.
93   *Manual*, trans. Johnson, p 315.
94   *History of Philosophy*, Vol III, p 219.
95   See Masson, *Recent British Philosophy*, (1865), cited in Aarsleff,
'Locke in the Nineteenth Century', *Monist*, Vol 55, No 3, July
1971, esp. p 401.
96   See e.g. Kuno Fischer, *Geschichte der Neueren Philosophie*, Vol
I. 1855, trans. Gordy as *Descartes and his School*, New York,
1887, pp 160-61.
97   *The Problems of Philosophy*, HUL, 1912, pp 114-5.
98   *Ibid.* p 115.
99   *Human Knowledge, its Scope and Limits*, London, Unwin, 1948,
p 172.
100 *Locke, Berkeley and Hume*, OUP, 1931, p 8.
101 For a striking account of the effect of neo-Kantianism on studies
of the history of philosophy in France, see Bréhier's 'La Notion
de Renaissance dans l'Histoire de la Philosophie' (see above, n 6).
102 On the idea that Hegelianism had dominated philosophy,
particularly at Oxford, see Collingwood's *Autobiography* (OUP,
1939), pp 15-17.
103 'Descriptivism', *Proceedings of the British Academy*, 1963;
reprinted in W. D. Hudson (Ed.), *The Is-Ought Question*,
London, Macmillan, 1969, p 240.
104 *A Critical Exposition of the Philosophy of Leibniz*, pp xi-xii.
105 In this context, 'historical knowledge' means inquiry into
individual situations, whether past, present or future, and not
only knowledge of the past. In this sense the opposite of
historical knowledge is general or universal knowledge, such as is
provided by mathematics or the theory of electricity or of logic.
106 On such boundaries see Michel Foucault, *The Archaeology of
Knowledge*, (1969) trans. A. M. Sheridan-Smith, London,
Tavistock, 1972, esp. pp 21-30.
107 Of course it is possible to discuss beliefs which have never
actually been held; but in order to identify them one needs to
locate them in a hypothetical or fictional historical context.
108 See above, p 11.

Chapter Two

ANALYTICAL PHILOSOPHY AND THE HISTORY OF PHILOSOPHY

by

Michael Ayers

It is often thought that philosophers have a legitimate interest in the works of the past which is quite distinct from the interest of intellectual historians. Consequently it is fruitless to charge much of the philosophical commentary used in our universities with being unhistorical or even inaccurate. What must be criticised, if criticism is to gain a foothold, is the attitude that sees those properties as no fault.

This seems worth doing simply in the name of objectivity. There is as yet no convincing understanding of 'progress' or other comprehensive pattern in the history of philosophy. The appearance of orderly progress often owes its existence precisely to the capacity and tendency of philosophers to make use of the theories and words of their predecessors for fresh purposes, only loosely linked to the old ones. But those who do advance comprehensive theories of the history of philosophy are at least talking about something which should be of interest, and must be of importance, to philosophers.

It is possible that those who disclaim an interest in the history of philosophy betray in the shortcomings of their understanding of the past, some of the limitations of their own philosophical theories; above all their theory as to what is of significance in philosophy. In this respect the misinterpretation of popular texts is as revealing as the neglect of unpopular ones. While it is true that the tradition chiefly studied in British philosophy departments in recent years has been too narrow, I shall restrict my argument to the more positive vice.

Some historians have recently called for greater objectivity and historical sense in the history of philosophy. John Dunn has eloquently described the conflict that arises between the desire to achieve an historical understanding of the genesis of a text (the intentions of its author and its meaning for its original readers) and the desire to use it for one's own philosophical purposes. Quentin Skinner, Hans Aarsleff, and others have similarly explored the methodological sources of misinterpretation.[1] The more extended and forceful of these discussions, however, have concentrated on political philosophy, where the connection with the history of events is most intimate. I shall try to extend the argument to general philosophy, where the issues are not exactly the same and, in particular, where the problem of meaning is more insistent.

Russell on Leibniz

The notion of a 'purely philosophical' attitude to the history of philosophy is an old one, but one that is peculiarly well-fitted to the analytical philosopher's conception of philosophy as 'logic' and utterly distinct from the time-bound contingent facts of psychology and history. It is no accident that the attitude finds emphatic expression in those influential remarks at the beginning of Russell's early work on Leibniz.[2]

Russell begins by distinguishing his own concern for the truth and consistency of doctrines from an interest that others may have in questions about 'the influence of the times and of other philosophers' which 'require for their answer a considerable knowledge of the prevailing education, of the public to whom it was necessary to appeal, and of the scientific and political events of the period in question.' Strangely, he sometimes seems to have believed it possible to pursue these latter questions lacking a clear knowledge of what the philosopher under consideration actually believed: 'an influence may be established by identity of phrase, without any comprehension of the systems whose causal relations are under discussion.' We may thus suspect that the motive of Russell's 'purely philosophical attitude' is the desire to dissociate himself from a kind of 'history of philosophy' of which few could consciously approve. And yet the imputation that certain sorts of historical knowledge are in principle irrelevant to his own enterprise goes much further than that.

At the same time he takes note that 'the problem as to the actual views of the philosopher who is to be investigated' is, 'after all, perhaps the most important of the historical questions';[3] allowing that, in the case of Leibniz at any rate, the setting forth or 'reconstruction'[4] of the philosopher's system may be a demanding task. When this initial chore has been completed, Russell felt, the commentator should point out and prune away[5] those inconsistencies of doctrine that resulted from extrinsic or accidental considerations such as the desire to maintain an appearance acceptable to prevailing religious opinion. Thus, 'we, who do not depend upon the smiles of princes, may simply draw the consequences which Leibniz shunned.'[6] The discovery of more fundamental inconsistencies, deriving from the acceptance of basic premisses apparently compatible but in reality conflicting, together with the assessment of each premiss and the reasoning behind it, constitute the philosophically interesting part of the enterprise and, for Russell, its end.[7]

Of these three stages in the commentator's task—that of giving an organised account of doctrine, that of removing impurities unimportant to their author and lastly, the stage of philosophical evaluation of the result—the first is described by Russell himself as historical and the second must be presumed to be historical at least in part, since it embodies hypotheses about an individual's psychology. Yet Russell believes that both can be settled without any 'considerable knowledge' of history. Even in the case of Leibniz, Russell ascribes the difficulty of exposition to Leibniz's public reticence, so that the obstacle can be overcome simply by reading the esoteric writings and seeing logical connections between the opinions publicly and privately expressed. There is supposed to be no such barrier 'in the case of most philosophers,'[8] and a contrast is drawn with the explicit geometrical order of Spinoza's *Ethics*.[9]

The tendency of Russell's whole discussion of methodology is vastly to underrate the difficulty, or at any rate the laboriousness, of the 'historical' parts of the commentator's task. Understanding a philosophical work involves understanding the intellectual forces and purposes that it embodies, and there would have been little chance of understanding Spinoza's potentially very mysterious achievement had it come down to us from an age of which we were otherwise ignorant. For there would have been little chance, even by way of speculation, of hitting upon correct hypotheses as to the philosophical point, if not the verbal meaning, of his neat, technical definitions, axioms and theorems.

In the absence of wider historical sources, our own philosophical intuitions will inadequately fill the gap. We shall tend to read the philosopher as if he shares, not our principles perhaps, but our preoccupations, our presuppositions as to which issues are fundamental. As Jonathan Rée has suggested above, Russell's assumption that the expositor's task is relatively straightforward seems connected with his belief that there exist in some Platonic heaven a few 'great types of possible philosophies' which are accessible to pure reason and to which we can presumably refer directly when in need of an interpretive hypothesis. What is unintelligible in these terms will then necessarily appear unworthy.

Certain general properties of Russell's own performance are sufficient to raise doubts about his methodology. Russell's Leibniz is motivated by a few, for the most part 'logical' beliefs, of which perhaps the most fundamental is a prejudice in favour of analytic subject-predicate propositions, and from which the rest of his system can be derived.[10] As Russell sees it, Leibniz's philosophy 'begins', like 'all sound philosophy', 'with an analysis of propositions.'[11]

This dependence is presented as if it were psychological as well as logical: the order is not treated as one imposed on Leibniz by Russell himself for the sake of neat exegesis, nor even as the logical order ultimately achieved by Leibniz in pursuit of some Euclidian ideal, but as the order in which Leibniz actually thought. Thus his doctrine of the unreality of independent relations is supposed to have been formulated because 'he is unable to admit, as ultimately valid, any form of judgement other than the subject-predicate form.'[12] In his popular works, it is held, Leibniz disguised the dry and abstract roots of his system, deliberately misrepresenting it to the public view as a pleasing religious picture.

Against such an interpretation, it may be argued that Leibniz did not derive an ontology from a logic independently regarded as indispensable, so. much as hammer out a logic appropriate to an ontology or world-view which attracted him for other reasons. If this opposition is too crude, it is so partly because of the crudities necessarily involved in departmentalising philosophy, but also because Leibniz thought in the context of philosophies in which logic, philosophy of science, epistemology and theology already had certain relations to one another and to ontology or metaphysics. The aim of finding where his philosophy 'begins' is largely misconceived. Nevertheless the historical perspective itself strongly suggests that, however much logical considerations came to influence him, his ontology was less a deduction from unargued logical presuppositions, than a response to contemporary problems in the philosophy of science and philosophical theology. For example, the rejection of spatial and causal relations should be seen against the sceptical paradoxes currently drawn from the nature of extension and the difficulties raised in relation to the interaction of mind with body.

The fundamental ontological concept of the time, the concept of substance, had been reshaped by the new science. This movement was accompanied by attacks upon the infatuation with logic, and consequent deception by language, to which faults in the science of the Scholastics were often ascribed. Leibniz himself says that the definition, 'when several predicates are attributed to the same subject and this subject is not attributed to any other, it is called an individual substance' is 'not enough, and such an explanation is only nominal.' We must have recourse to 'the nature of things.'[13] Individual substances, for Leibniz, are the ultimate subjects of *explanatory* discourse: their ontological ultimacy is tied to their 'intelligibility'. They are ultimate subjects because a full understanding of reality would depend on knowledge of their natures or essences. In attributing this sort of intelligibility to finite individuals Leibniz opposed the philosophical mainstream since Plato. One consequence was that he could readily treat general laws of nature as contingent, and as admitting miracles as exceptions. Moreover, the full intelligibility of things became transcendental, beyond the reach of human science. We need not suppose that this profound metaphysical move was determined by a preconception of the logical form of propositions. Certainly his motives were far distant from the sort of concern with a question whether individuals have essences that we are likely to find in a modern work on 'logic' or 'semantics'.

If these suggestions are even approximately correct, Russell has directed us onto the roundabout of Leibniz's system at the wrong place. His mistake is itself historically significant, since, in arriving at his conception of Leibniz, Russell evidently found confirmation of his conception, perhaps still being formed, of the nature of philosophy and of its fundamental problems. Here is a demonstration of one interconnection between pure philosophy and the history of ideas. Because our own theory of philosophy may help to determine our understanding of another philosopher, of his motives and aims, it can at the same time be confirmed, or appear to be confirmed, in so far as that interpretation is plausibly presented. The *a priori* can thus receive a kind of confirmation or rebuttal from the historical, and that is one reason, not the least important, why philosophers, for their own good, should not despise the struggle for historical accuracy.

Philosophical Truth and Historical Distortion

Euclid's ideas can be given a place within our mathematics independently of the circumstances of their origin. Ideas in metaphysics, logic and epistemology, even if more evidently controversial than mathematical ones, can seem to share the same independence of the accidents of history. This illusion deserves examination.

At one point in his book, *The Political Thought of John Locke*,[14] (from which the example is unfairly drawn) John Dunn discusses Locke's claim that it is impossible to change men's beliefs by political coercion and that religious belief must therefore fall outside the scope of political authority. Dunn remarks that it is 'difficult to see why Locke found his own argument so convincing.' But, he says, in the historical context it 'was a plausible extrapolation from the religious and political history of England over the preceding thirty years.'

Yet elsewhere Dunn quotes a passage in which Locke offers the different but concordant argument that political authority, since it is by definition a right transferred from the governed to the government, can only extend to actions within the citizen's own power: 'Now that a man cannot command his own understanding or positively determine today what opinion he will be of tomorrow is evident from experience and the nature of the understanding, which cannot more apprehend things otherwise than they appear to it, than the eye see other colours in the rainbow than it doth.' Thus Locke's position, while failing to allow for the real possibilities of manipulating men's beliefs, coincides with his very important rejection of the Cartesian doctrine that assent is an act of will. That issue, undiscussed by Dunn, is still worth discussing and even, perhaps, worth relating to the question of 'freedom of belief'. Dunn's historical explanation may be apposite, but Locke's doctrine has a life independent of a particular thirty years of English history.

A full historical explanation should, of course, allow for such philosophical connections, and the influence of Descartes' *Meditations* is as 'historical' as the influence of political events. But it may seem possible to concentrate our critical attention on philosophical connections in total abstraction from, indeed in perfect ignorance of, any historical circumstances that made it attractive to a particular Englishman to draw *this* conclusion from *these* premises. It may seem possible to approach such connections, as Russell says, 'without regard to dates or influences.'

It is also important that there can seem almost to be a moral obligation, by pretending that long dead philosophers 'sit round the same table' as the living, to prevent the reduction of thought to its origins. There exists an attitude that is not only unhistorical, but anti-historical. It is perhaps expressed by H. H. Price when, in *Hume's Theory of the External World*,[16] he addresses his book 'to those who write about Hume as philosophers, not as mere historians of philosophical literature: to those who ask what his statements mean, and whether they are true or false, and what consequences they entail.' Price has 'nothing to say' to those 'who inquire into the historical genesis' of Hume's opinions. Forty years after Russell, Price even more emphatically attributes to the unaided philosophical intelligence the power to uncover 'meaning', and clearly shares Russell's contempt for a crew condemned to grub about on questions of genesis, whose highest achievements will doubtless consist in showing that philosophers universally admired got their ideas from philosophers hitherto unrecognised. Such hostility has its source, in part, in a desire to preserve from historical explanation a role for purely (who would dare say 'merely'?) philosophical thought.

This sense of opposition between 'mere' history and philosophy is surely an illusion, but one, perhaps, which can only be dispelled by actual examples of insights gained and errors avoided in an inquiry in which they are complementary. When Dunn states as a *desideratum* of his kind of 'historical account' that it should be made possible to see 'that in the circumstances that prevailed, the *Two Treatises* was the work that Locke would have written,'[17] it is easy to imagine the wincing reaction of those for whom any philosophy worth the name must transcend the circumstances of its authorship. Yet Dunn's own performance, in which by holding up the text against the historical possibilities he brilliantly illuminates its actual philosophical meaning, provides the best justification of his enterprise. For there then seems little virtue in a 'purely philosophical' approach to thoughts that no-one ever had, in 'solemnly and expertly flailing thin air.'[18]

We can, it is true, oppose Russell's model of the timelessly subsisting 'great types of possible philosophies' with a picture of the history of philosophy as the history of man's or, rather, individual men's continuing struggle to make full sense of experience. Philosophy has not been a long, isolated conversation in a universal language on the same identifiable topics. Philosophers have not all quarried at the same mine so that we can measure against our own 'purely philosophical' judgment how much logical truth each has carted away. Yet that sort of generalisation ultimately rests on its being more difficult than Russell would have us believe simply to understand particular philosophical texts.

The distortion involved in the 'purely philosophical' approach cannot, of course, be avoided merely by being more 'historical'. No methodology can rule out mistakes, or make it impossible that pre-conceived theory should dictate a misleading record of fact. Like a philosopher, an historian may be too much influenced by what he feels a writer ought to have meant. The point is that the distortion perpetrated by a philosophical commentator should be regarded in just the same light, with the same disapproval as the distortion of an historian.

When C. B. Macpherson portrays Locke as a self-conscious and rather savage bourgeois ideologist[19] the truth is obviously important, since we can only feel that, if he is right about Locke's meaning, his Marxist theory of history has received a piece of crude confirmation. If, on the other hand, it is as Dunn suggests, and the neat fit between Macpherson's data and his theory is achieved only by his ignoring some of the more obvious features of the actual context within which Locke wrote (most notably, perhaps, the fact that Locke's argument was a reaction to Filmer's doctrine of Divine Right, not an attack on the working class,) Macpherson's theory has not indeed been refuted, but a particular application of it as a theory of interpretation has been deprived of force.

The same is true when the theory of interpretation against which the data are viewed is abstract and 'philosophical' rather than 'historical'. If our philosophical instincts tell us that a writer is trying to express a certain abstract principle or is guilty of a certain conflation or confusion, that too is an historical judgment. There seems, indeed, to be a vast confusion behind much 'history of philosophy' itself: its practitioners evidently find it congenial to point to historical object-lessons in support of their conception of philosophy, and yet wish to be as invulnerable as possible to refutation by arguments which draw on all the kinds of historical evidence and reasoning that may be necessary or helpful in determining what a man actually meant, and why he said what he did.

This confusion characteristically expresses itself in an ambiguous attitude towards the commentator's task. Russell,

when he advocated the removal of accidental complications
from a theory so that the 'main doctrines' should stand clear for
philosophical evaluation, did not consciously countenance
historical inaccuracy. Price, however, often seems to see the
point of selection and simplification differently, not as a
preliminary historical chore, but as an heuristic exercise in
philosophy. Rather than using Hume as an Aunt Sally, 'always
taking him exactly at his word', we should 'give him a fair run
for his money': 'When he makes mistakes, we must try to get
him out of them, by suggesting other alternatives which he
might consistently have adopted. We must try to go behind his
language, and when he is obscure . . . we must try to make him
clear. That is the spirit in which the works of Kant are
commonly studied. "What he really meant," we say, "is
perhaps not quite what he said". . . We try to restate Kant's
doctrines in modern terminology. We stretch them a little, so
that they may be able to accommodate the subsequent
developments of Physics or Psychology or Logic . . .
Contrary to the precepts of Kantian ethics, we must use our
illustrious predecessors as means, not as ends: as means to help
us to understand the world, or to analyse our experience, or to
clear up our linguistic muddles, or whatever the aim of
philosophical inquiry is thought to be. (After all, if we can use
them so, it is really the highest compliment we can pay
them.)'[20]

Bold, generous and 'relevant', the programme can hardly fail
to evoke a cheer. We might ask, however, what Price means by
'mistakes', and how we are to identify them. Not every doctrine
or inference with which we disagree can be a 'mistake':
otherwise every writer would be 'got out of' his mistakes into
the critic's own opinions. Price does not express agreement
with his modernised Hume. Clearly some distinction is
assumed between important and unimportant mistakes, like
Russell's between two sorts of inconsistency.

But should our criterion of importance be what mattered to
Hume, or what matters to ourselves? If the latter, the result will
largely depend upon 'whatever the aim of philosophical
inquiry is thought to be' and may well be worthless from the
point of view of history or an interest in Hume's meaning. If the
former, then the way is open for the point that only with

historical knowledge could an hypothesis as to Hume's fundamental purposes and problems be adequately established.

Price, like most analytical philosophers and whatever he
says in theory, maintains in practice an uneasy ambivalence
towards historical fact, as if trying to reconcile these two
notions of a 'mistake'. An example of this attitude is provided
by his characterisation of Hume's treatment of the idea of
identity as a 'serious mistake' calling for correction. For Hume,
the very notion of identity through time and change is
incoherent, consequent upon a self-contradictory fiction of an
irrational faculty, the imagination. Price, not surprisingly,
rejects this conclusion, but also feels free to help Hume out of it
by radically revising the argument. The justification for this
move, of which the details are unimportant, is that 'by revising
Hume's analysis of Identity, which is in any case inconsistent
with the main principles of his philosophy, we can contrive to
abbreviate the "considerable compass of very profound
reasoning" which caused him so much trouble; and we can
contrive to offer a much simpler and more credible account.'[21]
Thus Hume is being helped to say what, with a clearer head, he
would have wished to say.

As it happens, the accusation of inconsistency is
unconvincing, while the revised account is doubtfully
compatible with Hume's principle, surely 'main', that ideas are
copies of impressions. Yet is it not in any case a curious
procedure by which Hume himself is called upon as an ally
against his own conclusion and transmuted from a philosopher
who, quite characteristically, accuses a fundamental concept of
being incoherent, to one who accepts a certain explanation of
its coherent content? Is it not rash to assume that a passage,
apparently designed to trouble the reader, troubled its author
in the same way? Or to suppose that Hume would have
preferred a 'simpler' explanation than his own of our belief in
independent objects? Or that an eighteenth century sceptic was
trying to appear 'credible' to a reader with the notions of
Oxford two hundred years later?

Yet here we may feel that Price is motivated by something of
a quite different order from the desire to help Hume to express
himself: namely, a determination to find in Hume a
'constructive' theory, in order that he may be 'used'

constructively. For, so Price tells us, his aim 'is to bring out the positive and constructive side of Hume's teaching, rather than the destructive side, which he stressed himself.' Moreover, Hume allegedly 'made a serious mistake at a critical point in his argument', which 'can be corrected' so that 'his constructive doctrine can then be developed a good deal further, without sacrificing any of the fundamental principles of his philosophy.'[22]

The principle that the commentator can and should correct 'mistakes' when the result is 'constructive' has a certain moral odour but might seem an odd one to apply even as an heuristic principle to the work of a philosophical sceptic. It is hardly a plausible rule for helping such a philosopher to be himself. Nevertheless Price skirts the main methodological issue, never getting it clear whether he is merely using Hume's scepticism as the starting-point for the construction of a different, unsceptical theory on modern lines, or whether, in discounting or changing the more sceptical arguments, he is trying to reveal a constructive 'doctrine' or 'side' which is embedded in the *Treatise* and to which Hume himself can properly be supposed to have been attracted at least some of the time.

If it is really felt that the commentator is justified in making what he can of a text in accordance with his own view of philosophy, it is surely muddled also to suppose that the result was mysteriously there before he started. Since most analytical philosophers speak from the horns of this dilemma, it is not surprising if their methodological pronouncements are more often than not a bit odd.

The Historical Methodology of Analytical Philosophy

A principle of the analytical movement is the belief that a gulf exists between traditional philosophers and ourselves such that we now have, not merely new theories, but virtually a new discipline. At the same time the past retains a manifold relevance, and a certain view of it is an important ingredient of the new enlightenment. In *Language, Truth and Logic*, A. J. Ayer writes of the principle of verifiability, 'There is no need for us to give further examples of the operation of our criterion of significance. For our object is merely to show that philosophy, as a genuine branch of knowledge, must be distinguished from metaphysics. We are not now concerned with the historical question how much of what has traditionally passed for philosophy is actually metaphysical. We shall, however, point out later on that the majority of the "great philosophers" of the past were not essentially metaphysicians and thus reassure those who would otherwise be prevented from adopting our criterion by considerations of piety.'[23]

The distinction between 'analysis' and meaningless 'metaphysics' promises to turn the history of philosophy into a procedure of sifting wheat from peculiarly inconsiderable chaff. It might well seem beneath a philosopher's dignity to go very far into the history of mere confusion. On the other hand, Ayer actually spends little longer in praising Berkeley for having recognised that 'it must be possible to define material things in terms of sense-contents, because it is only by the occurrence of certain sense-contents that the existence of a material thing can ever be to the least degree verified,'[24] than he does in locating the source of 'Locke's discredited assumption of a material substratum'[25] in 'the primitive superstition that to every name a single real entity must correspond.'[26] Much 'metaphysics', although 'without literal significance', is thus diagnosed as false analysis of language.

Logical positivism serves, indeed, as a general psychological theory as to how philosophy, good and bad, comes to be written. At the same time it tells us that, as philosophers, we need only concern ourselves with those aspects of a thinker's work which the theory seems capable of explaining, i.e. which can be attributed to linguistic insights or linguistic confusion. Ayer himself believed that the greater part of metaphysics could be blamed on such 'humdrum' muddle, although he left a little room for other, 'poetic' motives.[27]

The same impression is generated by the other writings of about this time or a little later that helped to constitute 'linguistic' philosophy. Although Wittgenstein, in particular, was less inclined than Ayer to see plain truth in some traditional doctrines, there was general agreement that a renovation of philosophy could be achieved by new methods which would enable us to identify and to avoid the linguistic misconceptions supposedly embodied in the very idea of the old systems. That, indeed, has been the point of the linguistic approach. Yet, although such writers as Wittgenstein, Wisdom, Ryle and even Austin give us to feel that they are dealing, in their different ways, with the real reasons why philosophers say what they do, we find in them little or no discussion of historic arguments, not to speak of systems of thought. Doctrines are generally identified by means of brief and often abusive caricatures.

A number of those who formed the next generation of analytical philosophers probably saw in this openly careless, generalised treatment a shortcoming or, at least, an opportunity missed. Book-length studies of the great philosophers continued to be in demand. Hence there has arisen a *genre* of commentary produced by authors ready to work through a system doctrine by 'still interesting' doctrine, 'theme' by 'theme'. Such commentary, not surprisingly, is strongly imbued with the attitudes earlier exemplified by Russell and Price, together with a particularly lively sense of the necessity of selective reshaping and 'translation'. Price's objection to Aunt Sallies seems not, however, always to be shared.

A prominent and in its way highly impressive example of this type of commentary is the work of Jonathan Bennett, which is presented as the application of 'modern analytical techniques' to old questions. He believes that 'we understand Kant only in proportion as we can say, clearly and in contemporary terms, what his problems were, which of them are still problems and what contribution Kant makes to their solution.'[28] On its natural interpretation, this statement implies that there can be no such thing as understanding a philosopher in his own terms as something distinct from, and prior to, the difficult achievement of relating his thought to what we ourselves might want to say. How Kant or (to involve more perspicuous writers in the sample) Berkeley or Descartes understood their own words without benefit of modern analytical techniques is not explained. It is a more straightforward view that understanding Berkeley is not different in kind from understanding Bennett. A prerequisite in each case is some knowledge of the writer's intellectual situation, whether gained by reading musty volumes or by breathing the air of British and American philosophy departments.

The programme of flattening the past into the present in the name of understanding it, is one that will have greater appeal the more certain we are that we are now in a position to clear up the muddles of our predecessors. It is nevertheless unsurprising to find P. F. Strawson praising the method for heuristic virtues apparently independent of that complacent assumption: 'Bennett's Kant is not a giant immersed, or frozen, in time. He is a great contemporary . . . with whom we can all argue . . . ; and so Bennett does argue . . . and summons to join in the argument . . . those older contemporaries, Locke, Leibniz, Berkeley and Hume, and those younger contemporaries, Wittgenstein, Ryle, Ayer, Quine . . . This is splendid, and a necessary corrective to that extraordinary isolation in which Kant tends to be islanded, partly indeed, by his own unique qualities, but partly by oceans of the wrong kind of respect.'[29]

We may reasonably wish to know whether this singular and emphatic denial of time springs from a belief that all philosophers are genuinely contemporaries under their skins, or from a fear that our students will fall asleep. For unless the former belief is true, we may be losing something of philosophical value when we try to discard all sense of distance, or when we forget that that with which we are trying get into critical relationship comes, after all, from the past. Piety is doubtless dispensable, but it need not be unduly respectful towards those philosophers to feel that a prerequisite of *seriously* reading Leibniz or Berkeley, not to speak of Plato, as contemporaries, would be the skin of a rhinoceros. It is at any rate doubtful whether we should as readily as Bennett telescope the two tasks, distinguished by Russell as by common sense, of understanding a philosophical position and judging its worth.

One popular concept that serves to obfuscate this last distinction is that of 'reconstruction' or, somehow more ominously, 'rational reconstruction'. Perhaps Russell's view that 'an influence may be established by identity of phrase' finds support here, but when *he* talked of the 'reconstruction' of Leibniz's system he meant little more than the orderly

presentation of relationships that its author was supposed to
have chosen to leave inexplicit. The current use of the word as a
term of art is better illustrated by a recent typical, if otherwise
innocuous, piece in the journal *Mind,* on 'Mill's Proof of the
Principle of Utility'.[30] Its author, Neil Cooper, does 'not wish
to discuss here what Mill "really meant", but only to see
whether his proof can be reconstructed as a valid argument
with the minimum of reinterpretation.' His aim is 'to
"reconstruct" an argument which a too facile criticism has
rejected as invalid.'

Cooper does not say that the consideration of what Mill
'really meant' is worthless or impossible, although the scare-
quotes suggest something of a wild goose chase. He does,
however, make two characteristic assumptions. The first is the
presupposition that, by modifying a doctrine so that it can be
supposed to convey a truth, we are somehow only doing justice
to its author. Yet the tendency of such a method is to reduce the
stature of almost any philosopher to whom it is applied. For his
doctrines will be presented as a set of disconnected, partial,
obscurely expressed insights, rather than, as it might be, an
idiosyncratic but reasonably coherent, if to us incredible,
whole.

I do not want to suggest that all worthwhile philosophies are
perfectly coherent, and there is doubtless a sense in which none
has achieved or even closely approached full 'coherence'. But
there is a danger that what Dunn calls the 'struggle for
coherence' should be lost from view, when this struggle is
arguably what is most important in the philosophical
enterprise. The danger is not lessened by the piecemeal
approach of much analytical philosophy, which is often held
together in the individual by no more than some general view
of the nature of philosophy, or some preferred analytic method
which can be applied to this distinct problem or that. Indeed,
the isolation of 'problems' for individual treatment is often,
overtly or in effect, a major part of the method.

The second assumption of Cooper's position is that it is
possible to produce a version of a philosopher's argument
purged of any incidental 'obscurities, if not confusions', as he
puts it, without first discovering what the philosopher 'really
meant'. This brushing aside of the problems of exegesis, which

invites the question how one can recognise a 'reconstruction' unless one bothers to read the original, is sometimes supported by an argument, an extreme statement of which occurs in D. J. O'Connor's book, *John Locke*.[31] For O'Connor, there is no point in discussing 'what Locke "really meant" ' since 'nobody but Locke himself could give such an account, and he is dead'! Thus it is pointless to 'claim an interpretation to be "correct".' This does not matter, however, since 'what interests his readers is the extent to which his actual words excite their interest in philosophical thinking and suggest lines of thought that will help to elucidate their own philosophical puzzles'!

Even in the sphere of 'art' the notion of an 'intentionalist fallacy' is dangerous and over-used, but to try to apply such a notion within philosophy is, if anything is, a betrayal of reason. To an unsympathetic eye, the recommendation appears to be this: 'If an argument of a dead philosopher puzzles you, rewrite it as any argument that you can think of which looks moderately like the original, but which does not puzzle you. Without bothering further about that philosopher (although, like O'Connor, you will continue to talk as if you are describing his "views",) praise or criticise the result. You will be safe from the charge of anachronism, because you are a philosopher, not an historian. In any case, misinterpretation can never be proved.'

The notion that words have an entirely independent life, odd as it is, crops up elsewhere.[32] Perhaps Bennett's concern with 'what is happening in Berkeley's pages'[33] reflects a similar conception. More explicitly, Alan Ryan contrasts the historical approach, which, he says, 'may yield the historian a coherent and convincing answer to the question of what Locke *really meant,*' with his own concentration on the text. An account based solely on the text 'may perhaps be in danger of refutation by the historian as an account of *what Locke intended*. It is in less, even no, danger of contradiction from such a quarter as an account of *what Locke said.*' Ryan appeals to our alleged practice of holding 'people to what they say, rather than to what they may suppose to follow from what they meant to say.'[34]

The notion of holding people to mere words powerfully underestimates the possibilities of ambiguity and misunderstanding. O'Connor wisely reserves such irritating treatment for the dead. Yet the possibilities of misunderstanding are not less if we have to do with a technical conversation which took place long ago; particularly if we insist on attending only to a selection of the most prominent participants, and only when they can be taken to be discussing topics that already interest us.

What We Have Lost

The programme of modernisation and 'translation' is plainly useless to anyone other than a philosopher. It is less well recognised that it can involve considerable philosophical loss.

Some hint of the possibility appears even in Ayer's allusion to a Berkeleian 'analysis' of material object statements.[35] It is true that for Berkeley physical reality consists in a class of immediately perceived 'ideas' or, in Ayer's terminology, 'sense-contents'. But it does not follow that he would define the class of 'material things' without reference to anything except sense-contents. As he explains his notion of physical reality, it is 'the ideas imprinted on the senses by the Author of Nature' that 'are called *real things*.'[36] His doctrine, with its essential reference to God, does not, and in consistency could not, rest on the simple verificationist argument ascribed to him by Ayer, for Berkeley held that our knowledge of God and other spirits depends on a justified inference from our own 'ideas of sense'.[37] We should thus need strong independent evidence before attributing to him the principle that it must be possible to define Xs in terms of Ys whenever it is only by the occurrence of Ys that the existence of Xs can be verified. There is no such evidence. Berkeley links word-meaning with 'experience', which includes our awareness of our own essential spiritual activity, but nowhere links sentence-meaning with verification.

Ayer's version of Berkeley was not novel. It reflects the dominant twentieth-century conception of *the* problem of the material world, indeed the dominant conception of 'epistemology'. This conception centres on the question of how belief can justifiably extend beyond immediate experience. A few years before Ayer wrote, C. R. Morris had flatly asserted the amazing falsehood that only in occasional minor arguments does Berkeley treat the notion of 'material substance' as self-contradictory, while 'his chief effort is directed towards showing that there is in fact nothing in experience to justify belief in its existence.'[38] For Ayer, moreover, Berkeley's phenomenalism must be supposed to be both separable from theism and derived from something like the allegedly clinching modern argument for phenomenalism, if it is to be praised as an analytic insight. Hence Berkeley is turned into a verificationist without God.

Even if we agree that theism is philosophically dead, we cannot conclude that whatever is of positive value in Berkeley will exclude reference to God. Few assertions of importance made by that often incompetent straw figure, Berkeley without God, are made with the same meaning by the historical Berkeley. What is rejected makes a difference to what is retained. One of the most famous sentences he wrote may serve as an example: 'The table I write on, I say, exists, that is, I see and feel it: and if I were out of my study I should say it existed, meaning thereby that if I was in my study I might perceive it, or that some other spirit actually does perceive it.'[39] The hypothetical clause '. . . if I was in my study I might perceive it' is often treated in isolation as a kind of flirtation with the principles of modern phenomenalism. Yet it is a forerunner of the modern theory only in a much looser, hardly more than causal, sense. Not only does Berkeley have 'some other spirit' up his sleeve as continuous perceiver of what we do not perceive continuously, but his whole conception of hypothetical fact centres on his notion of God's causal activity and laws or 'set rules'. These underlie natural powers and possibilities as the explanatory essences of substances were taken to do on the rival doctrine of Locke. There is no evidence that Berkeley contemplated, even momentarily, a theory like Ayer's, in which hypotheticals, interpreted perhaps as mere predictive rules, supply the ultimate ontological explanation of unperceived existence.

It is thus a mistake to pick out, as Bennett has done,[40] those sentences or even parts of sentences from Berkeley's writing that could have been written by a modern phenomenalist, as if they represented a separable 'vein' manifested in Berkeley's writing. We must contrast, not just words and phrases, but their meaning within different systems. Such a comparison need not be to the advantage of the modern theory. Even in the case under discussion, it can bring into focus the peculiarity and weaknesses of the Positivist conception of hypothetical facts. On the other hand, if we choose to make discussion of Berkeley relevant to more recent concerns by pretending that within his theory a modern phenomenalism is occasionally struggling to get out, the modern theory will inevitably appear superior, if only on the score of clarity and consistency.

Another consequence of modernisation may often be tedium. Nothing is more designed to make the history of philosophy boring than the unrelenting search for primitive forms of modern theories, or for naive blunders that modern theories can be praised for correcting. The complexity and the difference of the original are qualities not lightly to be sacrificed for the sake of wholesome, but familiar lessons.

When Berkeley tells us that the *esse* of sensible things is *percipi,* while that of spirits is *percipere,* he is doing something odd but interesting with a traditional notion of the 'being' of things. He is applying to the relationship between mind and matter the conception of hierarchically related categories of existence or ontological levels. Spirit is a 'substance', which 'exists' in the primary sense; sensible things are 'accidents' or 'dependent beings.' The ontological substance/accident relation is identified with the perceiver/object relation. The notion of different senses of 'exist' owes its place in the argument to the argument's relation to a tradition. All this is at the heart of Berkeley's idiosyncratic metaphysics, yet G. J. Warnock, writing on the *esse* is *percipi,* tells us nothing of it. Instead he finds Berkeley 'generally perplexed by the notion of existence' and attributes to him a puzzled line of thought, of almost comical naïvety, which becomes the occasion for a disquisition by Warnock on that not neglected topic, whether existence is a property.[41]

The notion of 'translation into modern terms' can provide an even quicker route to banal and irrelevant criticism. It is tempting to endeavour to understand any technical term, such as the term 'idea', by translating the sentences in which it appears into ordinary language or some preferred modern terminology. Very often, if anything resembling sense is to be retained in each instance of its use, the term will naturally be replaced by different expressions on different occasions. Thus Locke's 'ideas' may sometimes be translated as 'concepts', sometimes as 'sensations', 'sense-data' or 'sensory states', sometimes, perhaps, as 'intentional objects' and so forth. It seems to follow either that the term is, as Ryle puts it, 'ruinously ambiguous',[42] or that its use is based on the gross conflation of obviously different things.

Yet Ryle in 1933 listed five senses of Locke's term, while O'Connor in 1952 produced a different list, which indicates the weakness of the charge of vicious ambiguity. For as such differences reflect philosophical differences between commentators, so the charge of ambiguity does no more than announce the critic's differences from Locke. Instead of holding Locke's terminology up against that of our own theories, we should try to understand his purposes in relating thought and sensation as he does.

For the linguistic philosopher, of course, the confusions allegedly revealed by such 'diagnoses' of equivocation may not at all seem 'humdrum'. Bennett, for example, can imbue his revelations with the excitement of a detective story. Berkeley has confused the notion of 'substance' with the notion of 'matter', he alleges, and the 'conflation' is attributed to a 'double use' of the term 'idea' to denote both sensible qualities and sensory states. This 'double use' is then itself perceived to have an occult origin not manifest in Berkeley's arguments. We are told that, because Berkeley follows Locke in holding that to have in mind the meaning of 'white' is to have in mind an 'idea', in the sense of an image or sensation, of white, and because thinking of the meaning of white may be equated with thinking of the quality whiteness, the term 'idea' comes unnoticed to mean for him quality as well as sensation. Thus we arrive at an even more fundamental 'double use' of 'idea': everything can be laid at the door (in a phrase itself not without duplicity) of the 'underlying assumption that the word 'idea' can be used univocally to cover something in the nature of sensory states and something in the nature of concepts or meanings of words.'[43]

The distance we have travelled from the text lends an air of profundity to the explanation, and it can only be gratifying to a philosopher of language to be told that Berkeley's trouble has its source both in his theory of meaning and his linguistic confusion. On the other hand it may seem to us perverse to ignore Berkeley's very different, frequent, open and interesting arguments against the ontological distinction between sensible qualities and our perceptions of them. Berkeley is, indeed, no more guilty of equivocation than, say, Descartes is in arguing against a real distinction between space and matter, and so against a vacuum.

An object of even greater distortion and trivialisation than the theory of ideas is the traditional doctrine of substance. Much discussion of it is close in spirit to Ayer's criticisms of 'primitive superstition' and the 'unreflecting analysis' of ordinary beliefs, 'which takes the grammatical structure of a sentence as a trustworthy guide to its meaning.' Bennett finds reason to criticise Ayer on substance, but he himself offers us this 'rational reconstruction' of a 'certain line of thought' which Locke admittedly did not 'adopt', but 'entertained':

> What concepts are involved in the subject of the statement that *The pen in my hand is valuable*? Certainly, the concepts of being a pen and of being in my hand; but these are not all, for the statement is about a *thing which* falls under these two concepts. What thing is this? It is the purple thing which I now see; but when I say that the purple thing I now see is a pen and is in my hand, I speak of a *thing which* is purple, etc., and so I have still failed to capture the whole concept of the subject in my original statement . . . What will be missing from any list of descriptive concepts is the concept of 'a thing which . . .' . . . This constituent of every subject-concept is the concept of a property-bearer, or of a possible subject of predication—let us call it the concept of a *substance*. So, if any existential or subject-predicate statement is true, then there are two sorts of item—substances, and properties or qualities.[44]

Locke's philosophy of science is one of the most important in human history, and his concept of substance has an essential role in an ontology devised for, and springing from, his philosophy of science. Bennett, however, in his eagerness to 'reconstruct' Locke's point as a purely logical one, concerned with linguistic structure, has chosen a significantly inapposite illustration. The relevant part of Locke's discussion concerns the 'simple ideas' involved in our definitions or 'complex ideas' of specific substances, such as *gold* or *man,* and of general substances, such as *matter* and *spirit.* Those definitions, Locke argues, are always in terms of 'observable' natural properties, i.e. sensible qualities and experientially ascertainable 'powers', which must be supposed to have a basis in, and to flow from, something else, an unknown underlying nature. It is this supposition that is, he thinks, reflected in the form of the definitions: 'as body is a *thing* that is extended, figured and capable of motion.'[45] Yet 'The pen in my hand is valuable' is not even a definition, but a contingent statement about a particular. The property of being valuable is not even a natural property. It is difficult to imagine a deeper level of incomprehension, or a more effective barrier to our receiving profit from Locke's thought.

It has seemed best, if not without risk, to include in my argument some abbreviated discussion of particular questions of interpretation that I have myself treated at greater length and, it is to be hoped, less inadequately elsewhere.[46] Yet examples could be multiplied almost indefinitely by drawing on most discussions, of whatever intellectual quality, which promise to use modern philosophical insights or 'techniques' to unravel the history of thought. It seems to be inevitable that such procedures will cut us off from important and unusual ideas. It may be as unfortunate, even from a 'purely philosophical' point of view, that they tend to cut us off from our past.

We can hardly philosophise without some conception of our relationship to our predecessors. Such a conception may be overtly historical or more purely logical as in the case of most analytical philosophy, which sees past thought as a useful ragbag of logical insights and confusions. J. J. Katz's judgment that philosophy has been 'puzzling about words for over two thousand years', and that only a general theory of language such as Chomsky's will save us from 'endless quibbling' over particulars,[47] is extreme but characteristic. Sometimes, however, a more historical note is struck. Michael Dummett attributes the 'revolutionary importance' of Frege's work to its 'displacing the theory of knowledge from the position which

Descartes had given it, as the base of the entire subject, and replacing it, in this role, by the theory of meaning.' He accordingly predicts that 'for, say, another two centuries', 'it is with linguistic philosophy that philosophical progress lies.'[48] Yet whatever form the analytical philosopher's understanding of the past may take, it can deserve respect only so far as it is coupled with a readiness to take the history of ideas seriously as a complex, but objective discipline. We shall not know what we have lost, or gained, if we do not trouble to be right about the meaning of what we have inherited.

Notes

[1] See John Dunn (1) 'The Identity of the History of Ideas', *Philosophy*, 1968. Reprinted in P. Laslett and others (Eds), *Philosophy, Politics and Society: Fourth Series* (Oxford, 1972), (2) *The Political Thought of John Locke* (Cambridge, 1969); Quentin Skinner (1) 'Meaning and Understanding in the History of Ideas', *History and Theory*, 1969, (2) 'Motives, Intentions and the Interpretation of Texts', *New Literary History*, 1972 (3) " 'Social Meaning' and the Explanation of Social Action" in Laslett and others (Eds), *op. cit.*; Hans Aarsleff (1) "Some Observations on recent Locke Scholarship" in J. W. Yolton (Ed.), *John Locke: Problems and Perspectives* (Cambridge, 1969), (2) "Cartesian Linguistics: History or Fantasy?", *Language Sciences*, 1971, (3) "Locke in the Nineteenth Century", *The Monist*, 1971. But see also Maurice Mandelbaum's very recent, more general discussion, 'On the Historiography of Philosophy', *Philosophy Research Archives*, 1976.

[2] *A Critical Exposition of the Philosophy of Leibniz* (London, 1900) pp xif.

[3] *ibid.*

[4] *id.* p 2.

[5] *cf. id.* p xii.

[6] *id.* p 3.

[7] *cf.* pp xii, xiv, 4.

[8] *id.* p 2.

[9] *id.* p 1.

[10] *cf. id.* pp 4 *et passim.*

[11] *id.* p 8.

[12] *id.* p 13.

[13] *Discourse on Metaphysics* trans P. G. Lucas and L. Grint (Manchester, 1953) sect. VIII.

[14] (Cambridge, 1969) p 33.

[15] *id.* p 40 footnote.

[16] (Oxford, 1940) p 3.

[17] *op. cit.* (2) p 9.

[18] *id.* p.x.

[19] In *The Political Theory of Possessive Individualism.* (Oxford, 1962) Ch.V.

[20] *op. cit.* pp 3f.

[21] *id.* p 50.

[22] *id.* p 10.

[23] 2nd ed. (London, 1946) p 40.

[24] *id.* p 53.

[25] *id.* p 126.

[26] *id.* p 42.

[27] *id.* p 45.

[28] *Kant's Analytic* (Cambridge, 1966), back cover.

[29] "Bennett on Kant", *Philosophical Review,* 1967.

[30] *Mind,* 1969.

[31] 2nd ed. (New York, 1967) p 13.

[32] Roy Edgley has pointed out to me that this kind of view receives perhaps its fullest theoretical expression in Karl Popper's theory of 'objective knowledge'.

[33] 'Substance, Reality and Primary Qualities', reprinted in C. B. Martin and D. M. Armstrong (Eds.), *Locke and Berkeley* (New York, 1968), p 122.

[34] 'Locke and the Dictatorship of the Bourgeoisie', *id.* p 232. My criticism is limited to Ryan's methodological remarks. It is, of course, sometimes possible to rebut an interpretation by reference to the text alone.

[35] See footnote (24) above.

[36] *Principles of Human Knowledge* Part I § 33.

[37] *id.* §§ 145-155. Berkeley's whole argument needs to be seen in the light of this elegant piece of natural theology, its climax.

[38] *Locke Berkeley Hume* (Oxford, 1931) p 74.

[39] *op. cit.* Part I § 3.

[40] *Locke, Berkeley, Hume: Central Themes* (Oxford, 1971) pp 145f etc.

[41] *Berkeley* (London, 1953) pp 197ff.

[42] Gilbert Ryle, "John Locke on the Human Understanding", reprinted in Martin and Armstrong (Eds.), *op. cit.*

[43] Martin and Armstrong (Eds.), *op. cit.* p 94. The explanation is retracted at *Locke, Berkeley, Hume,* p 74, but I am here interested in the approach which it exemplifies.

[44] *Locke, Berkeley, Hume,* pp 59f.

45 *Essay Concerning Human Understanding,* II. xxiii 3.
46 See M. R. Ayers (1) "Substance, Reality and the Great, Dead Philosophers", *American Philosophical Quarterly,* 1970, (2) "The Nature of Things", *Philosophy,* 1974, (3) "Locke on Power and Substance", *Philosophical Quarterly,* 1975.
47 *The Philosophy of Language* (New York, 1966) pp 92f, 286f.
48 Letter to *The Listener,* January 1974.

Chapter Three

HEGEL'S 'HISTORY OF PHILOSOPHY'

by

Adam Westoby

Hegel's *History of Philosophy* is, among other things, a work of philosophy; and has a specific historical position.

Hegel was born in 1770. He was 18 when the Bastille was taken and 23 when Robespierre went to the guillotine. In 1806 he completed the *Phenomenology of Mind* and in 1816 the first version of the *Science of Logic*. In 1818 he was appointed a professor at Berlin, where he stayed until his death just over a year after the July 1830 revolution in Paris; and was subsequently academically 'embalmed' as head of Germany's reigning philosophical school.

His *Lectures on the History of Philosophy* were first given at Jena in 1805-6 and repeated twice in Heidelberg in 1816-1818. Six further full courses were given in Berlin, from 1819 up to the eve of his death in 1831. The 1805 series was prepared shortly before he began writing the first part of his philosophical 'system', completed as the *Phenomenology* in October 1806. For these first lectures Hegel wrote out a full manuscript. Subsequent changes took the form of annotations, and marginal and miscellaneous notes, except for the long Introduction which was completely re-written in October 1820, for presentation in Berlin. The Introductions, both of 1805 and of the 1820s, agree in awarding the palm of knowledge to philosophy, whose exponents have 'won for us by their labours the highest treasure, the treasure of reasoned knowledge'.[1] (HP, I, 1) The lectures, therefore, although they predate the first published work of Hegel's maturity, the *Phenomenology,* fall quite definitely within (and in their successive deliveries virtually span) the period after about 1801 in which he devoted his energies above all to questions of philosophy.

Hegel regarded himself as the first philosopher to prepare a systematic and comprehensive account—as opposed to a compendium—of the history of philosophy up to his own time. For this absence of precedents Hegel provides the core of an explanation early in his Introduction. Previous philosophers proclaimed their own absolute truth, and saw their relation to *their* predecessors in this light alone:

> each one in turn comes forth at first with the pretext that by its means all previous philosophies not only are refuted, but what in them is wanting is supplied, and now at length the right one is discovered. (HP, I, 17)

Philosophers, concerned with the certain knowledge of general truths, saw in the variety of philosophies evidence that their forerunners had, with greater or lesser ingenuity, failed, or only partially achieved, this common and unchanging goal. This did not discourage the best of them from seeking it in their turn, but it acted as a powerful disincentive to work on the history of philosophy. History became, for philosophy, the antechamber to the dustbin.

Hegel strongly disagreed with this attitude. It is, he said:

> really important to have a deeper insight into the bearings of this diversity in the systems of Philosophy. Truth and Philosophy known philosophically, make such diversity appear in another light from that of abstract opposition between Truth and Error. The explanation of how this comes about will reveal to us the significance of the whole history of Philosophy (HP, I, 18-19).

The rational history of philosophy thus forms a necessary element of the science of philosophy.

This is so not only in the general sense that previous philosophies are themselves a necessary part of the Idea (the culminant achievement of consciousness, in which mind fully recognises both the external world and its own peregrinations as parts of its achievement of complete self-consciousness) but also in the stronger sense that the historical order of philosophies corresponds to 'the sequence in the logical deduction of the Notion—determinations in the Idea.'

(HP, I, 30). Only an 'absence of philosophic mind' could portray the history of philosophy so that 'the succession of its systems are represented simply as a number of opinions, errors and freaks of thought.' (HP, I, 31)

Hegel's demand for a philosophical approach to philosophy's past is connected with the fact that he lived through a particular turning point of European history—and that, as the Preface to the *Phenomenology* makes clear, he was conscious of doing so.[2]

At the end of the eighteenth century, Europe came to the boil. Though it was in France that the bubbling was fiercest, the headiest vapours were in Germany—products of the latent heat released by the enlightenment as it transformed itself into radicalism and romanticism, which have now dispersed. Pre-eminent among those which condensed into a more permanent form was Hegel's philosophical work, which remains a powerful source of turbulence (though less so within English philosophy), not least in that it is still the subject of division among Marxists. Such a powerful present influence inevitably encourages one to 'suspend criticism and concentrate on exegesis'.[3] This I have tried to avoid, but only by bearing in mind an injunction typical of Hegel: that the truth is concrete. I therefore take a few particular examples treated in the *History of Philosophy,* selecting them in part for their interest in themselves, but mainly for the features which they reflect as 'thought objects' encountering Hegel's method.

The truth is not only concrete, according to Hegel, it is also 'the whole'; the conflict of these two aspects lies at the centre of its contradictory character.

This essay seeks also to respect the second maxim, in that it attempts to concentrate on elements that are central to Hegel. No writing on Hegel can by-pass the nature of his work as a whole, so often does he insist that science is science only *as system,* that particular knowledge can be understood only as part of a whole which has, finally, no determinate boundaries.

Hegelianism, after Hegel, divided itself, if one may oversimplify, into adherents of the system and of the method. Dialectical materialism claimed and developed the rationality in the method, while the system (in its original form) atrophied and died in the hands of official philosophy. But even in modern interpretation an antagonism often makes itself felt between Hegel's treatment of particular empirical material and the *dialectical method* which he employs both in locating it within his overall system, and as the key to its own being and alteration. Professor Findlay, for example, says of the lectures of the later years:

> Hegel's empirical spirit seems to range in barefoot delight over the broad fields of beauty, worship and speculation, quite freed from the pinch and creak of the dialectical boots.[4]

Hostility to the dialectical method remains a potent intellectual force; it has both social roots and an intellectual momentum which make it probably more powerful, and certainly more articulate and elaborate, than it was in Hegel's time. Nonetheless, it was a resistance whose universality Hegel clearly recognised—and opposed—as we see with particular clarity in his treatment of Heraclitus and of Kant.

Every new generation must try to redigest the past, transforming the substances of which it is composed and drawing from them the nourishment which its own inner appetites demand. This is especially true of Hegel. Ever since his own time he has exercised a fascination rivalled only by his inaccessibility. Heine, for example, knew him personally, and greatly admired him, yet his *Religion and Philosophy in Germany*,[5] which contains so much that is perceptive on German idealism, and relates it so precisely and wittily to the political eruptions of the time, only deals with Hegel briefly and allusively—even though his closing section is entitled 'From Kant to Hegel'. He regards the mature Hegel as a renegade, an 'apostate to his own doctrine' who has 'slunk back to the religious kennels of the past'[6], but what exactly this 'greatest of all philosophers begotten by Germany since Leibniz'[7] is a renegade *from* he never makes clear. Marx's *Grundrisse*[8] for *Capital* make it clear what an effort was required of him to convert the 'rational kernel' of Hegel to the analysis of the categories of capitalism. Lenin also felt the need in 1914, when he could already detect the labour pains of the European revolution, to take up a thorough study of Hegel's *Science of Logic* (to which he added a reading of substantial parts of the *History of Philosophy*). His notes[9] make it clear how much he felt he had gained from this work, but at the same time how far he was from being able to present a definitive account for publication.

If these examples warn us of the difficulties of an approach to Hegel, they should also convince us that attempts to come to grips with him are worthwhile. For years within the official Communist movement his importance has been obscured. The widening of interest in the last few years among Marxists and socialists is in part a reflection of the sharpening of class relations and the consequent ideological crisis of Stalinism and its intellectual fellow-travellers. A new generation has sought to broach many problems of philosophy and logic, of the theory of knowledge, of interpreting the history of society and human thought; tasks for which Hegel is in many matters the starting point.[10]

The present essay is of a very limited scope. It attempts to provide, from the standpoint of Marxism, an interpretative introduction to Hegel's *History of Philosophy*. At certain points I indicate in what way Hegel's treatment provides the key to an objective understanding of developments, and elsewhere I try to identify an essential limitation of his approach. But these indications, in such a brief essay, fall far short of an *assessment* of either Hegel or the history of philosophy as a whole. Nonetheless, it is important to say— even if schematically—what may be grasped by focusing on the *History of Philosophy,* and how.

It is first necessary, though, to deal briefly with Hegel's account (in his lengthy Introduction) of what philosophy is and (a closely connected question) how its history is ordered. In a note to the *Encyclopaedia Logic,* the crucial correspondence between the history of philosophy and the development of the logical Idea is stated with great explicitness:

> In the history of philosophy the different stages of the logical Idea assume the shape of successive systems, each based on a particular definition of the Absolute. As the logical Idea is seen to unfold itself in a process from the abstract to the concrete, so in the history of philosophy the earliest systems are the most abstract, and at the same time the poorest. (EL, 159)[11]

What is suggested is not merely a correspondence of the order, but that the history of philosophy is one of progress in the direction of more comprehensive rationality.

Earlier philosophies, Hegel continues in the same passage:

> are preserved in the later; but subordinated and submerged. This is the true meaning of a much misunderstood phenomenon in the history of philosophy—the refutation of one system by another, of an earlier by a later. (EL, 159)

Yet something is forced in this correspondence with the Logic. In the same note Hegel claims that:

> logic begins where the proper history of philosophy begins. Philosophy began in the Eleatic school, especially with Parmenides. (EL, 160)

yet the *History of Philosophy* properly opens with Thales. Two things should be noticed: firstly, that Hegel is tempted more than once to identify another 'real' start for philosophy; and secondly, that in this instance there is a clear reason for setting aside Thales (for whom water is the essence of all things) and selecting Parmenides (with his doctrine that Being is the absolute) as the 'proper' commencement of philosophy, since this will permit an exact fit with the opening of the *Science of Logic*—'*Being, pure being,* without any further determination.' (SL, 82)[12]

But what, according to the Introduction, is 'philosophy proper' and how may we identify its beginning? It is, at its simplest, 'Mind's thought of itself' (HP, I, 45). Mind faces the result of its previous labours—

> an heirloom to which all the past generations have added their savings . . . . and which they had won from the depths of Nature and of Mind. (HP, I, 3)

and the given object is taken to be worked upon and transformed in its turn.

> On the presupposition of an already existing intellectual world which is transformed in our appropriation of it, depends the fact that Philosophy can only arise in connection with previous Philosophy, from which of necessity it has arisen. (HP, I, 3-4)

These abstract premises imply a more fundamental ambiguity of the 'beginning'. But Hegel does single out two more definite conditions as necessary for the commencement of philosophy—one material and the other spiritual. Materially,

> cravings of want must have disappeared, a strength, elevation and inward fortitude of mind must have appeared, passions must be subdued . . . Philosophy may thus be thought a kind of luxury, insofar as luxury signified those enjoyments and pursuits which do not belong to external necessity as such. (HP, I, 51)

On the other hand, philosophy can only arise in a people for whom a gulf has already arisen between the strivings of their mental and moral life on the one hand and their day-to-day life on the other. The 'kingdom of thought' must have removed itself into opposition with 'the world of actuality'.

> When Philosophy with its abstractions paints grey on grey, the freshness and life of youth has gone, the reconciliation is not a reconciliation in the actual, but in the ideal world (HP, I, 52)

These conditions first arose among the early Greeks. But, apparently paradoxically, Hegel stresses how the natural 'at-homeness' of Greek life was *equally* part of the preconditions for the birth of philosophy. Sketching the attitude of modern man he indicates that 'what makes us specially at home with the Greeks is that they made their world their home' (HP, I, 150), and describes how they generated for themselves, in their myths

> all aspects of their existence, such as the introduction of fire and the offerings connected with it, the crops, agriculture, the olive, the horse, marriage, property, laws, art, worship, the sciences, towns, princely races, etc. Of all these it is pleasingly represented through tales how they have arisen in history as their own work. (HP, I, 151)

The two descriptions in fact are not inconsistent. For they have annulled the 'foreign nature' of their origins only by imaginatively recreating their own origins, representing 'their own existence as an object apart from themselves, which manifests itself independently and in its independence is of value to them.' (HP, I, 151). It is this, mankind's life, seen as conscious, purposive and moral, becoming an independent object of thought, which is the essential precondition for 'Mind's thought of itself' to begin.

And this 'prehistory' of philosophy is echoed within Hegel's own intellectual career. If we accept that his life may be divided (at about 1801) into 'youth' and 'maturity', we may perhaps characterise the periods as follows: the young Hegel concentrated on problems of ethics, of social custom, and of religion with the intention of making a 'scholar's contribution' to the practical improvement of human life; at this time the Greek ideal of social harmony and the original moral teachings of Christ are in the foreground, while Kant and his successors receive less attention.[13] For the mature Hegel, however, the crisis in philosophy and the criticism of philosophy is central— the correct solution of ethical and social problems is accessible only on the basis of a scientific philosophical system. Thus, while the *Life of Jesus* (1795)[14] modernises Christ as a preacher of the categorical imperative, the Introduction to the *Phenomenology* (1806) centres round a logical and philosophical assault on Kant's arguments for the unknowability of the 'thing-in-itself'.

In and after 1801, therefore, Hegel made a 'turn' to philosophy and, as the Jena manuscripts testify, one of his self-imposed tasks (after the Jena essays of 1801 on the 'critical philosophy')[15] was a comprehensive study of the history of philosophy.

When he claims a close parallel between the development of philosophy in history, and of the logical Idea, it is vital that we understand that Hegel wrote his Logic after a study of the history of philosophy rather than writing that history within the already-formed conceptual framework of the Logic. This biographical fact expresses an essential determination of Hegel's philosophy. He insists, against his predecessors, that logic is a product of human history. And, as an idealist, he views this history as essentially the progressive development of spirit.

How, then, may one summarise what can be gained from a study of Hegel's *History of Philosophy?* In philosophy, human thought is simultaneously at its most general and powerful, and at its most rigidly constrained. In philosophy it reflects— whether knowingly or not—the working of consciousness itself, and therefore the material world and practical activity only at a further remove. The history of philosophy displays, thus, directly the development of self-consciousness, less directly the development of consciousness, and more remotely still the development of the practical and material world. Each of these connected facets is present—and each to a certain extent consciously so—in the *History of Philosophy*. One of my aims is to demonstrate this. Another is to outline the relations which Hegel sees between these facets. And a third is to show, in specific form, the principles of development and self-movement—dialectics—which Hegel sees at work both in thought and in the world.

I have tried to achieve these aims by means of examples—inevitably giving a partial picture, but one I hope which illuminates essential points:

1   With *Thales* and his Milesian successors Hegel identifies philosophy as such, and also the origin of the concept of 'matter';

2   With *Heraclitus* he deals with the first statement of general laws governing movement and becoming—primitive dialectics;

3   *Socrates* represents for Hegel philosophy first turning with full consciousness on itself, in the form of reflective morality;

4   In his treatment of *Kant,* Hegel attempts to resolve the crisis of philosophy in his own time, and goes simultaneously in search of his own immediate origins.

The last section returns, in the light of these examples, to Hegel's general method, to the plan of his *History of Philosophy,* and to some of the contradictory elements which are to be found within it.

Thales

In the *History of Philosophy* Hegel identifies Thales of Miletus as the first real philosopher.

Hegel is concerned to show that the whole essential achievement of philosophy is contained—as a kernel—in Thales' assertion (and the arguments for it conjecturally attributed to him by Aristotle) that water is the one universal substance. The important thing is not that Thales singles out water as such, but that he withdraws from all the variety and changeability of the objects of knowledge to discover a single and unchanging universal, which gives rise to the sensuous world as the different forms of its essence; and, of equal importance to Hegel, that this concept of unity within all the variety 'defined water to be the infinite Notion, the simple essence of thought.' (HP, I, 185). For the first time consciousness addresses itself to the world not as something independent of it which it must understand in the forms in which it appears, but as in some measure its own creation.

Recent historians of philosophy generally agree with Hegel that the Milesian cosmologists were the pioneers of philosophy—but disagree as to what their essential innovation was. Guthrie's detailed *History*,[16] for example, lays stress on their exclusion of supernatural forms of explanation; it is not that the Milesians deny the existence of the gods, but that in their accounts of the origins or source of the universe gods do not appear. His emphasis is on the fact that, relative to primitive thought, this 'discovery of Nature' was an epochmaking intellectual step forward for man. This essential view is echoed by the Marxist writer George Novack:

> The Milesian criticism, or rather setting aside, of religious attitudes and ideas laid the foundation of philosophy and initiated the career of materialism.[17]

Hegel would not agree with this position. He claims that what distinguished Thales' assertion that water is the principle of all things is that

> with it the consciousness is arrived at that essence, truth, that which is alone in and for itself, are one. A departure from what is in our sensuous perception here takes place; man recedes from this immediate existence. We must be able to forget that we are accustomed to a rich concrete world of thought. (HP, I, 178).

and, later,

one must acknowledge that there is a great robustness of mind evinced in not granting this plenitude of existence to the natural world, but in reducing it to a simple substance. (HP, I, 179).

But this 'simple substance' is not treated as material; on the contrary Hegel paraphrases Thales' position that water is 'god over all'. The point is that

water, though sensuous, is not looked at in its particularity as opposed to other natural things, but as Thought in which everything is resolved and comprehended. (HP, I, 179).

Hegel regards the question of Thales' religious views as a secondary matter,[18] nor is he much concerned with the details of his attempts to derive, for example, mud and air as modified forms of water. The philosophic (and religious) significance of Thales lies in having constituted an abstraction in order to comprehend nature in a simple sensuous essence' (HP, I, 184) and in having 'defined water to be the infinite Notion, the simple essence of thought'. (HP, I, 184-5). If we leave aside for one moment the controversies labelled 'science versus religion' or 'materialism versus idealism', it is possible to see that Hegel is pointing to something of profound importance.

It is that Thales and the Miletans were the first to achieve an herculean effort of abstraction—the recognition of a *single* 'substance' or 'essence' in all the wealth and variety of nature. The establishment of this concept was more basic than the expulsion of supernatural beings from their accounts of the universe. In fact Hegel, the idealist, underlines the significance of a concept of 'matter':

with the ancient philosophers the principle has a definite and, at first, a physical form. To us this does not appear to be philosophic but only physical; in this case however, matter has philosophic significance. (HP, I, 180).

To the twentieth century, familiar in one form or another with controversies about philosophical materialism, the abstraction 'matter' seems natural. It is almost 'a matter of instinct' to subsume all the objects our senses perceive in a single category—which we accept as being in itself indeterminate as far as colour, density and so on are concerned. Such a mental attitude is a pre-condition both for any meaningful discussion of 'materialism' as a philosophical position, and of scientific attempts to discover the laws governing matter in general—physics and chemistry. But, effortless though it may be for us, this reflective 'stepping back' from the evidence of the senses, and the more limited abstractions dealing with particular types of objects, must have been an exceedingly painful and difficult step forwards in man's intellectual life. When, therefore, Hegel later quotes Cicero as reporting that Thales could not convince Anaximander 'that everything consisted of water' (HP, I, 185) we must understand the problem as attaching not to the 'water' but to the 'everything'. Within this 'everything', however, the distinction is not yet sharply drawn between mind and matter.[19] This is why it is false to attempt (as Novack,[20] for example, does) to recruit the early Milesians to the camp of materialism. This division within philosophy had not yet come into being.

Thales and his immediate successors can therefore claim to have been the first to grasp the need for a concept of universal substance which is not itself determined; Anaximenes took a step forward in basing his theories upon air which, for Hegel, has 'the additional advantage of being more devoid of form.' (HP, I, 189). But Hegel already points, in his discussion of Thales, to the fact that selecting any sensuous material, no matter how formless, as the basic substance, both creates and leaves unresolved the contradiction between the world conceived as an intelligible whole and the concrete variety of particular existences: 'Thus', he cautions, 'we approach the divorce of the absolute from the finite.' (HP, I, 179).

Heraclitus

This warning is a prelude to the enthusiasm with which Hegel greets Heraclitus; for it is at this point that philosophy first suceeds in dialectically uniting the determined and the undetermined.

> Heraclitus could not say that the primary principle is air, water or any such thing. They are not themselves processes, but fire is process; and thus he maintains fire to be the elementary

principle, and this is the real form of the Heraclitean principle, the soul and substance of the nature-process. Fire . . . is physical time, absolute unrest, absolute disintegration of existence . . . hence we can understand how Heraclitus, proceeding from his fundamental determination, could quite logically call fire the Notion of the process. (HP, I, 287).

Hegel's treatment of Heraclitus shows him at his most evidently partisan. It is both a celebration and a defence of the steps forward which Heraclitus took. This advance was not from Thales and his successors, but from Parmenides and the Eleatics,[21] for whom pure being, separated from all sensuous form, was the basic substance of the universe. Hegel reconstructs Heraclitus' philosophy from the relatively small number of reported 'dicta'—among which he places foremost 'the great saying: "Being and non-being are the same; everything is and yet is not",' (HP, I, 282), or, in a clearer saying ' "Everything is in a state of flux; nothing subsists nor does it ever remain the same." ' (HP, I, 283).

This 'necessity of becoming' therefore, is the 'fundamental determination' from which Heraclitus (in Hegel's inter-pretation) arrives at fire as both the essential substance of the world, and the quintessential expression of becoming itself.

There is also a definite sense in which Hegel sees Heraclitus, and not any of his predecessors, as the originator of philosophy.

> In Heraclitus we see the perfection of knowledge so far as it has gone, a perfecting of the Idea into a totality, which is the beginning of Philosophy . . From Heraclitus dates the ever-remaining Idea which is the same in all philosophers to the present day. (HP, I, 282).

This insistence on an intelligible totality he contrasts with Zeno's negative, paradoxical and sceptical dialectic: the external dialectic.

This view of Heraclitus as the true starting point is echoed in the *Science of Logic.* In the *History of Philosophy* Hegel writes:

> Here we see land; there is no proposition of Heraclitus which I have not adopted in my Logic. (HP, I, 279).

In fact a compliment to Heraclitus is built into the very structure of the *Science of Logic*. Chapter 1 ('Being') opens with two short paragraphs beginning respectively *'Being, pure being . . .'* and *'Nothing, pure nothing . . .'*,[22] (SL, 82) which demonstrate that as separate conceptual abstractions 'being' and 'nothing' are identical, indeterminate emptiness. From their 'vanishing' one into the other Hegel derives their 'truth . . . becoming, a movement in which both are distinguished.' (SL, 83). In the remark immediately following he credits 'the deep-thinking Heraclitus [who] brought forward the higher, total concept of becoming.' (SL, 83). The remainder of Chapter I treats of the moments of sublation of becoming— a sublation which is not an erasure, but a passage into the developed form of Chapter 2 in which both being and nothing are preserved: Determinate Being. Hegel's structural tribute to Heraclitus is thus expressed as follows. Being-in-general is the initial starting point of philosophy. But when this being is taken (as by Parminedes) in a state of philosophical immediacy, as a pure abstraction (the opposite of perceptual or physical immediacy) it is a truth formally contradictory to, and actually identical with, its opposite, nothing. Without escape from the chains of this absolute contradiction, philosophical progress is impossible. Thus the second 'point of departure' of philosophy must be found in a second creative leap of abstraction—first achieved by Heraclitus—which unites the absolute opposites with which the 'understanding' (as opposed to dialectical 'reason') of his predecessors had wrestled in vain—ending in the paradoxes of Zeno. Only thus can there be a scientific transition from these abstractions to a logic of 'determinate being'.

In this lies the clue to why Hegel praises Heraclitus for, so to speak, 'reifying' becoming, giving it a sensuous form as fire. At first sight it seems paradoxical—especially since Hegel himself, in treating of becoming in Chapter 1 of the *Science of Logic,* employs no such comparison, even as an aid to exposition. The explanation is that Heraclitus not only identifies and makes fundamental the abstraction of 'becoming'—he takes the first step beyond this to express the existence of becoming and determinate being—(albeit in a quasi-metaphorical way)—as fire, whose most striking 'determination' is its very lack of determinacy, its 'absolute disintegration of existence'. (HP, I, 287). Thus Hegel applauds the metaphor while still describing as 'deficient and contradictory' (HP, I, 288) Heraclitus' attempts to explain other sensuous substances as modified forms of fire.

If Hegel's exposition of Heraclitus seems obscure, it is not solely due to compression. Just as the minds of the early Greeks had to make a painful effort to arrive at the abstraction of one basic substance, so the minds of men in the twentieth century, for whom a belief in the stable identity of objects is part of the ruling mode of thought, must make an effort of science and will to recapture the universal presence of becoming. From one point of view the whole of Hegel's mature work can be regarded as an attempt, with all manner of devices, to lure the mind of modern Europeans from the clutches of the 'understanding' (as opposed to 'reason'), which in one form or another takes pure being to have substantive content.

Socrates

Hegel's approach to Socrates reveals some of the most important features of the *History of Philosophy* as a whole. There is a depth of engagement and enthusiasm that renders Hegel's own attitudes exceptionally clear. At the same time he displays his characteristic refusal to 'take sides' at the expense of an all-sided view. In the development of Hegel's own attitude to Socrates up to the cautious, pro-religious standpoint of the *History of Philosophy* we can clearly discern the transcendence of the 'young Hegel'. Above all the concern with contradiction and conflict expresses itself powerfully in both the content and the form of this section.

Hegel's treatment of Socrates is unlike his approach to any of the other philosophers included in the *History of Philosophy* in one important respect. In all other cases he gives a preliminary account, more or less detailed according as his sources and interest indicate, of his subject's life, and then goes on to discuss his doctrines. Any later reference back to the philosopher's life is generally episodic and incidental. But with Socrates his procedure is quite different. Socrates' life is, he assures us, 'closely intertwined with his interest in Philosophy, and the events of his life are bound up with his principles'. (HP, I, 389). Thus, throughout the section, events from Socrates' life are taken, not just as suggestive incidents, but as the expression of particular aspects of the philosophical Socrates. The famous trances are the form taken by 'the inwardness of consciousness'. (HP, I, 391). His sobriety at dawn, when all others are drunk, reflects

> no aimless abstemiousness and self-mortification, but a power belonging to self-consciousness, which keeps its self-possession in bodily excess. (HP, I, 395).

And in the details of his trial, condemnation and death Hegel discovers the very framework of Socrates' moral science. This method of treatment gives a form fully suited to the new content which Hegel sees entering philosophy at this point:

> the infinitely important element of leading back the truth of the objective to the thought of the subject. (HP, I, 386).

With Socrates the attention of philosophy to the personal subject is dramatically sharpened, and it concentrates upon the subject's tender spot, where it most keenly recognises itself as subjective: the point of individual moral decision and action.

From this point of view Socrates could not have advanced as a theorist without bringing the practice of his own life into accord with his teaching. Hegel's method of treatment therefore flows not from a contingent desire to make Socrates more vivid (though in fact he had, from his early youth, a keen interest in Socrates' life), but from the essence of his subject. Socrates was a man who lived, in his own person,

> a mental turning point [which] exhibited itself in him in the form of philosophical thought. (HP, I, 384).

In Hegel's view Socrates' strictly philosophical achievement was to have made concrete the conceptions latent in Anaxagoras, Protagoras and their followers—that thought is the universal principle—in the new form of the idea of the 'I', 'as the consciousness which rests in itself'. (HP, I, 385). Thus from Protagoras' general conception that everything that is known is permeated by thought, Socrates makes consciousness determinate, identifying the 'I' as consciousness which rests within itself, which makes external to itself the elements of movement and change, and which at the same time achieves a goal for this movement, the Good.

Specifically what Hegel's Socrates brought into the world was 'subjective' or 'reflective' (as opposed to 'objective' or 'natural') morality:

> The Athenians before Socrates were objectively, and not subjectively moral, for they acted rationally in their relations without knowing that they were particularly excellent. Reflective morality adds to natural morality the reflection that this is the good and not that; the Kantian philosophy, which is reflectively moral, again showed the difference. (HP, I, 388).

In pointing to the novelty of Socrates' concentration on the individual 'I', Hegel—almost in passing—makes a point of considerable significance: that the first philosophers started by analysing consciousness in general, and that it was a point of development beyond this to identify the single individual as its object. For much present-day epistemology and ethics—which in general take the individual as an automatic starting point— this may provide a warning as to the historical character of their own presuppositions.

Hegel insists that this shift to 'reflective' morality was not limited to philosophy, but on the contrary was a 'mental turning point' which found philosophical expression. This turning point is most clearly described in his account of Socrates' antagonistic relation to Athenian society; both at his trial and death at the hands of the democracy, and earlier as he was satirised by Aristophanes in *The Clouds*. Hegel regarded neither Aristophanes' jesting, nor the charges of impiety and of corrupting the youth of Athens, as unjust. Unlike many of Socrates' admirers[23] he does not pretend, on such matters, to any supra-historical standards which would allow him to take sides.

In *The Clouds* the Socratic dialectic, eroding the foundations of accepted standards, enables those who have learned it to do nothing more moral than trick and bemuse their more traditional neighbours. In anger, finally, a victim burns down Socrates' house. Hegel finds that Aristophanes dealt accurately with Socrates:

... we must admire the depth of Aristophanes in having recognised the dialectic side in Socrates as being a negative . . . For the power of judging in Socrates' method is always placed in the subject, in conscience, but where this is bad the story . . . must repeat itself. (HP, I, 430).

Hegel also finds proven the joint accusation against Socrates: that he sought to replace the Athenians' gods with new ones, and that he led the youth of the city astray from their duty of obedience to family and state. But on the first count Hegel interpolates a sophisticated justification of the charge. Socrates, he says, did not claim the existence of new gods but only of a new avenue to them, 'inward certainty', replacing the official oracles. But this 'inward certainty' is itself undoubtedly a god, making 'Socrates the hero who established in the place of the Delphic oracle, the principle that man must look within himself to know what is Truth'. (HP, I, 435). And the 'hero' was for this condemned correctly: in accordance, that is to say, with the spirit of the law. The condemnation was therefore no accident or stupidity but, in a sense which Hegel takes pains to explain, tragic. In what is truly tragic 'there must be valid moral powers on both sides which come into collision; this was so with Socrates.' (HP, I, 446). But if the moral weight of Athenian society was immovable, nonetheless the pressure of which Socrates was the forerunner proved irresistible. Individual consciousness and subjective freedom developed generally after Socrates' death, disintegrating the 'natural morality' of the city-state, and arousing also a posthumous sympathy for Socrates, so that some of his accusers were themselves put to death. The death and 'rehabilitation' of Socrates thus formed the final act in the tragedy of Athens. The social pressure of 'natural morality', and the rights of 'subjective freedom' proved absolutely irreconcilable, each destructive of the other. In his treatment of Socrates, therefore, Hegel poses the problem of social freedom and reason—the problem from which he started his development to philosophy, that preoccupied him in many passages of the *History of Philosophy,* and to which he attempted a solution in the *Philosophy of Right* (1821).[24]

The 'mental turning point' which Socrates expresses is therefore at the same time a turning point in Athenian social and political life. Yet it cannot be claimed that Hegel analyses this in the same way that, in some other passages,[25] he anticipates historical materialism in giving social transformations as the explanation of a step forward in consciousness. Philosophy is seen as the independent agent, which, through the trauma of Socrates' teaching, condemnation and death, transforms Athenian society. In this the treatment of Socrates typifies the general approach of the *History of Philosophy*—the idealist tendency to treat thought as the independent element,[26] the holder of historical initiative. The passage brings into focus the strength of Hegel's method— the ability to identify what is new in thought and the internal forces giving rise to it.

Yet there is a less direct sense in which Hegel does treat Socrates as the expression of social and practical life. Socrates the man lived his life in such a way as deliberately to embody his philosophical principles. His life and death therefore became, in large measure, free of the chance and accident which dominate most men, and were in a sense formed into a work of art. Though Hegel seems to compare Socrates at one point to a piece of sculpture,[27] it is in Greek tragedy that he finds the proper artistic form. What typifies Socrates' fate is that his misfortune is 'rational' because 'brought about by the will of the subject.' (HP, I, 446). This is what makes it tragic.

Tragedy is the form of art which most forcibly contains contradiction. Within the tragic situation mutually irreconcilable, equally necessary, forces are driven to their point of maximum antagonism, at which point there comes a necessary rupture, a crisis, and the destruction of the situation. Hegel's account of Socrates' trial shows him treating it with an emphasis on tragic development in order to give a living exposition of dialectic. Through the destruction of Socrates, the freedom of the subject is preserved, and the first nail driven into the coffin of unreflective 'natural morality'. Socrates becomes the most heroic of tragic heroes, knowing the forces with which he is coming into collision. In his refusal to compromise with the judges or to flee the prison where he awaits execution, he recognises the necessity of these forces and consciously propels the situation to its point of resolution. In this sense his individual choices become reasoned and universal. Like Christ, says Hegel, he 'gave up his individuality, but what was brought forth by him remained' (HP, I, 446)—the principle of 'self-creative reason' which the mature Hegel sees as the pulse of subsequent philosophy.

The comparison with Christ points to an important index of Hegel's general development. As he re-evaluates the relationship between Socrates and Jesus we can detect the progressive elevation of religious beliefs and values above human and social affairs.

At the age of fifteen Hegel had already noted his disagreement with one of his teachers over the interpretation to be placed on Socrates' last words. In the *Phaedo* Plato records that, when the paralysis of the hemlock had already reached his waist, Socrates said: 'Crito, we ought to offer a cock to Aesculapius. See to it, and don't forget.[28] (Aesculapius, son of Apollo, was the god of healing; it was customary to sacrifice to him when one had recovered from illness.) After this Socrates covered his face and soon died.

Hegel's teacher had suggested[29] that Socrates was already stupefied by the poison and did not know what he was saying. The schoolboy Hegel rejected this, suggesting that he was falling in with custom in order not to offend the feelings of the people. It seems reasonable to infer that Hegel already attached more than factual significance to Socrates' words. Socrates represented, in the German enlightenment and its return to the classics, the classical archetype of the enlightened man. Moreover, his teacher's suggestion is inherently implausible, in that its source is not a simply factual narrative, but one of Plato's rational reconstructions of Socrates' life and teachings. And in fact Hegel, during his youth, seems to be attempting his own reconstruction of Socrates and the significance of his last words—a reconstruction upon which the scarce factual evidence regarding the historical Socrates would have only a remote bearing. In 1786, for example, he notes a conjecture by Racine on the 'last words', that they were pleasantly ironic, implying no religious belief.[30] And then in 1793, as a young man of 23, he records his final interpretation, that it was Socrates' 'noble sense that he should thank the gods for his death, which he saw as a healing.' He denounces as 'the self-conceit of a sect' Tertullian's speculation that the cock was intended for Aesculapius' father, Apollo, who had prophesied at Delphi that Socrates would prove the wisest of all Greeks.[31]

Here, therefore, is an interpretation which suggests a noble and selfless Socrates, steady to the last in his mission of moral teacher and exemplar of the people. It also places Socrates' last words in harmony with the main body of the *Phaedo,* where he argues for the immortality of the soul. It thus suggests close comparison with Jesus—a comparison whose alterations during Hegel's life point up his development. The powerful increase, within this comparison of two human beings, of the contrast between Socrates' humanity and Christ's divinity, marks the older Hegel's retreat into mysticism, away from 'folk-religion' as the expression and cement of social well-being, to the 'rational' exposition of the Christian incarnation. In 1795[32] (though in an essay not intended for publication), Hegel compares Socrates' teaching and that of his followers with those of Christ in an entirely matter-of-fact way, contrasting the Apostles' attachment to the particular person of Jesus with the intellectual and political independence of Socrates' pupils. But in the lectures on the *Philosophy of Religion,* delivered during the last decade of his life, he draws an even closer comparison of Socrates with Christ, as both being teachers of men, only to overturn it on the grounds that 'The death of Christ is the central point round which all else turns.' Christ's *life* is only the 'outward history', which 'is for unbelief just what the history of Socrates is for us.'[33]

This elevation in Hegel's later years of the celestial Christ above the human Socrates reflects central changes: firstly, the rejection of a practical goal for philosophy as a component part of moral and social reform, for which Greece was to serve as the central ideal; and, secondly, the application of philosophy to the 'rational' justification of faith. Neither of these changes was ever wholly completed, but through the *History of Philosophy* runs a strand of argument in which the development of philosophy appears as preparation for the developed self-creative reason which will, miraculously, both be and know the Godhead of the late Hegel.

For the treatment of Socrates this has striking consequences. Socrates' death—almost an obsession of the young Hegel—is in effect glossed over. Though Plato's account presents 'a wonderful scene', it contains 'nothing very special.' (HP, I, 443). And though in the *Phaedo* 'the immortality of the soul is here first brought forward; yet it brings no consolation.' (HP, I, 443). Death is no healing, but an ordeal to be faced. Hegel seems deliberately to shy away from identifying the hemlock with the cross, the human with the divine. But, paradoxically, his increased deference to Christian faith seems to strengthen his treatment of Socrates. Far from being tempted by religious comparisons, he concentrates upon his subject as a moment in the development of human thought. It is true that he occasionally refers to 'the divine Socrates', but this has the sense of discovering the divine within the human, not of the word made flesh. Hegel views Socrates in a spirit of entirely secular idealism.

In Socrates, therefore, Hegel discovers reason embarking on its task of self-creation, as it turns its attention upon itself alone, and for the first time seeks goals (in the form of morality) for its own self-transformation. In one form or another (not necessarily that of morality) this attempt of thought to appropriate the world to itself is to be the basis for the development of modern philosophy.

Moreover, Hegel accurately identifies the separation of theoretical from practical activity as being the springboard of thought's attempts to 'pull itself up by its own bootstraps'. Socrates was part of a social group among whom

> the greater part of the day was passed without any particular business, in loitering about the marketplace, or frequenting the public Lyceum, and there partly partaking of bodily exercises, and partly and principally, talking with one another . . . Socrates also lounged about after this manner, and lived in this constant discussion of ethical questions. (HP, I, 396).

Socrates, Hegel points out, has no system—only a manner of dialectical intervention with others. His Socrates is very much a *re*construction—almost his own creation. In the moral goals of the Socratic individual Hegel identifies the attempt to attain a point of rest within the movement of thought: the first stepping-stone in the torrent which consciousness must cross once it gains the knowledge—or the illusion—of its own autonomy.

Kant

A stepping-stone is not, of course, a pedestal, but a point of unrest. The point of greatest unrest which Hegel identifies in the history of philosophy is Kant's 'critical philosophy'; and since it is the spot on which his own foot presses, it is also the immediate point of departure into his own philosophy.

For Hegel, Kant represents a shocking event, a philosophical point of crisis, a sort of cerebral equivalent of the French revolution.[34] The parallel is made explicitly:

> . . . the truth underlying the Kantian philosophy is the recognition of freedom. Even Rousseau represented the absolute to be found in freedom; Kant has the same principle, but taken rather from the theoretic side. The French regard it from the side of will, which is represented in their proverb: 'Il a la tête près du bonnet'.[35] France possesses the sense of actuality, of promptitude; because in that country conception passes more immediately into action, men have there applied themselves more practically to the affairs of actuality. But however much freedom may be in itself concrete, it was as undeveloped and in its abstraction that it was there applied to actuality; and to make abstractions hold good in actuality means to destroy actuality. The fanaticism which characterised the freedom which was put into the hands of the people was frightful. In Germany the same principle asserted the rights of consciousness on its own account, but it has been worked out in a merely theoretic way. We have commotions of every kind within and around us, but through them all the German head quietly keeps its nightcap on and silently carries on its· operations beneath it. (HP, III, 425).

There is, of course, a double identification here: of Kant with Robespierre—and of Hegel himself with Kant, both possessors of a 'German head'. The passage quite possibly inspires the comments of Marx[36] and Heine[37] on Kant's connection with the Great Revolution and on Hegel's covert revolutionary side. But however much as a middle-aged man Hegel dissimulated his political opinions, there is no doubt that what he greeted in Kant was the philosophical, religious and ethical iconoclast. The subject finds itself at its most alien from the independent world in which it lives, 'dualism is ultimate.' (HP, III, 453). 'I, as Reason or conception, and the things external to me, are both absolutely different from one another; and that, according to Kant, is the ultimate standpoint.' (HP, III, 455). In Kant, therefore, raised to an extreme point, is a tendency general to philosophy as a whole: the drive of human thought to separate itself from the world and render itself self-subsistent.

The 'infinite subjectivity' of the critical philosophy ends in an insoluble dilemma, taking the form of a demand that the existence of God (securer of good in the world) should be guaranteed by reason. But this demand being unsatisfied,[38] it is left to faith (and the *Critique of Practical Reason*) to bring the Almighty to independent existence.[39] Hegel reworks the demand—in his view the form taken by the basic impulse of philosophy—and moreover undertakes to satisfy it. As a preliminary to this he goes over the unreconciled contradictions which he discerns within the critical philosophy. Of particular importance is his attack on Kant's general project for a critique of the faculties of knowledge: the critical philosophy proposes

> first of all to supply a criticism of our faculties of knowledge; for before obtaining knowledge we must inquire into the faculties of knowledge. (HP, III, 428).

Knowledge is thus

> represented as an instrument . . . whereby we endeavour to possess ourselves of the truth. (HP, III, 428).

It seems that men must go looking for truth 'with spears and staves.' (HP, III, 428). Yet,

> to investigate the faculties of knowledge means to know them; but how we are to know without knowing . . . it is impossible to say. It is the old story of the scholastic who would not go into the water until he could swim. (HP, III, 428).

The reference to the 'scholastic' is one strand of a thread running through the treatment of Kant (and elsewhere)—the appeal to practical activity as solver of philosophical quandaries. 'Ordinary consciousness' rises above the dualism of subject and object, 'every action aims at setting aside a

subjective conception and making it into something objective.'
(HP, III, 453). Even 'the animal . . . practically brings about
unity' between itself and the things external to it.' (HP, III,
455). The insidiousness of the critical philosophy lies in the fact
that, in the modern spirit, it too appeals to practical utility.
When Kant proposes to examine knowledge as an 'instrument',
'to see whether it is capable of supplying what is demanded of
it' (HP, III, 428), the idea is plausible to the 'healthy human
understanding.' The irony of the critical philosophy is that its
'practical' proposals turn out upon analysis to be wholly
impractical, so much so that they seem to require of us the
logically impossible. Kant's philosophy is no aberration to be
put aside. He represents an impasse through which philosophy
must pass. Since for Hegel philosophy is an idealism,[40] striving
to make thought self-dependent, it contains, or heads towards,
a consciousness of impotence in face of the 'thing-in-itself.' In
the critical philosophy the impotence is absolute, to the point
where Kant denies the knowability of the 'thing-in-itself.'
Idealism, so to speak, castrates itself.

It is possible to see the whole of the *History of Philosophy* as
preamble to the problem posed by the critical philosophy.
Hegel has no solution to the problem; or, to be more exact, he
has two. On the one hand there is the appeal to practical life—
episodic and unsystematic, but nonetheless unmistakeable. In
this vein Hegel takes up Kant's discussion of the hundred
dollars of which existence is predicated.[41] 'That a hundred
possible dollars are something different from a hundred actual
ones is a reflection of a very popular nature' (HP, III, 453) he
sardonically agrees. This is why the point 'to which Kant clings
most strongly . . . that Being cannot be extracted from the
Notion' (HP, III, 455) has been so enthusiastically received.
But if a man really has 'so great a desire to possess a hundred
dollars' he must not stagnate in his imagination 'but push out
beyond it'—'he must put his hand to work.' (HP, III, 453).

More generally 'all activity is a conception which does not
yet exist, but whose subjectivity is abrogated.' (HP, III, 454).
Hegel's satire on the 'poverty of philosophy' is not, of course,
meant to suggest that philosophical problems can be rationally
disposed of by purely practical methods, but rather that
problems which stand in contradiction to practical experience

are one-sidedly posed, the products of a consciousness unable to overcome its own one-sidedness. Echoed, therefore, as a subsidiary theme in Hegel's later philosophy is the attitude of his youth towards the critical philosophy. While his fellow-students at the Tübingen seminary embraced Kant with unqualified enthusiasm, he kept his distance, and turned part of his efforts to the 'practical' question of a folk-religion for the people.[42]

But the dominant theme in Hegel's response to the crisis in philosophy is more abstract and more systematic. It sets out from an attack upon Kant as to the place of dialectics. For transcendental idealism 'contradiction has its source in our thought alone',[43] (HP, III, 451), whereas in fact contradiction is everywhere and a logic must be found to embrace it—a logic both of things and of thought. Kant's confinement of contradiction to the subject is congruent with his dualism; it is also a recipe for epistemological disaster:

> . . . Kant shows here too much tenderness for things; it would be a pity, he thinks, if they contradicted themselves. But that mind, which is far higher, should be a contradiction—that is not a pity at all. The contradiction is therefore by no means solved by Kant; and since mind takes it upon itself, and contradiction is self-destructive, mind is in itself all derangement and disorder. (HP, III, 451).

Mind can only find rest in the knowledge that all things become (the 'Heraclitean principle'—to which Hegel returns in the section 'Final Result') (HP, III, 545 et. seq.), that they both are and are not, that mind must grasp them as such and that it must consequently provide itself with a logic in which the law of non-contradiction is not absolute, in which opposites are also identical:

> Pure thought has advanced to the opposition of the subjective and objective; the true reconciliation of the opposition is the perception that this opposition, when pushed to its absolute extreme, resolves itself . . . To know opposition in unity and unity in opposition—this is absolute knowledge; and science is the knowledge of this unity in its whole development by means of itself. (HP, III, 551).

This is the 'resolution' behind the claim that 'actual Nature is an image of divine Reason.' (HP, III, 545). From this standpoint Hegel regards philosophy as complete, not in the name of a call to action, but because 'the world-spirit has at last succeeded in stripping off from itself all alien objective existence.' (HP, III, 551). In philosophy, mind examines the forms within which it knows 'alien objective existence', forms to which it often attributes 'objective existence' in their own right. Only by working through these forms can mind come to know that it has developed 'from itself what for it is objective.' (HP, III, 551). Hegel's escape from Kant is into the arms of God. Philosophy is resurrected as theology.

Hegel and historical materialism

The history of philosophy's progress is not smooth but a series of jerks. The impetus for each qualitative development is found, by Hegel, in the contradictions within a previous philosophical situation. In philosophy thought is at its most self-reliant. It distinguishes itself from religion, empirical science and practical activity by taking its own forms, concepts as its content. Because of this 'autonomy' the divorce between thinking and being can reach, in Kant, the status of a condition of rational epistemology.

Hegel unites being with thought. In this consists his truth. But he unites them idealistically. It is often said that it is in this that his falsity consists. He is visualised as suspended midway between Kant and communism. But to see it thus is to underestimate reason's cunning. The unity Hegel establishes is that of an absolute idealism: thought concludes by annexing nature and society to itself by overcoming the appearance—the necessary illusion—of its separateness and independence. The prelude to this is thought's reworking of itself, in the historical development of philosophy, in preparation for the task. To modern materialism his conceding primacy to thought appears false. In the world as we know it men and their thoughts fall under the sway of social and natural conditions which precede them and which they do not choose; this condition Hegel inverts. But this inversion is not a simple falsity. The goal of socialism is the creation of a society in which scarcity, the material domination of man by nature, and his mental domination by categories whose origin he does not know, are abolished. In communist society social man will be for the first time free of class limits, able consciously to develop his control over nature and over his own thought and emotions as part of nature.

From this standpoint Hegel's world-view may be seen to contain a vivid imaginary truth—as the inverted image of a world which must itself be turned upside down. Just as the value of a mathematical function may—having passed through reversals and discontinuities—approach a limit, Hegel's absolute idealism expresses a philosophical intuition of the goal towards which the conscious action of men will strive. This is not to suggest that idealism will supersede materialism; but both the 'autonomy of thought' in Hegel, and the wealth of intellectual development which has hitherto taken place within the framework of idealism, is something that communism, far from casting down, will realise for new purposes. In a classless and materially powerful society, human thought and feeling will set about deliberately reconstructing their own forms.[44] Being will determine thought afresh, for the first time through processes which are consciously grasped. In this sense man will become once again a natural being. Individual will and desire will take on a wholly new character under communism. Instead of presenting themselves as an external goad, the sources of emotions will be increasingly understood. Human will will be strengthened, not weakened, by the fact that its origins are no longer mysterious. One result of this change will be, for example, that the art of a communist society will be unable to resurrect the individual tragic hero. For the highest and most complex individuals will no longer be subjectively driven by hostile forces to their destruction; on the contrary they will realise what in Hegel's philosophy is only abstractly anticipated—right as an internal feeling and freedom as the expression of necessity.

With regard to Hegel's treatment of the history of philosophy this view of the kernel within his system has a double truth: not only does he achieve, in the absolute Idea, the inverted hieroglyph of a human world which is itself to be turned upside down—but he does so as the outcome of a

process of human thought working upon 'objects' within its
own domain and free of supernatural origins.

The outcome is of course not continuous with the process.
Between Kant's division of thought from being and the 'final
result' falls a chasm. Unable practically to bridge it, the
culminating moment of German idealism was yet able to
portray for us—even if 'mystically'—the other side. In order to
achieve the unity of thought and being, Hegel insists upon the
necessity of a dialectical logic—to 'know opposition in unity,
and unity in opposition'. (HP, III, 551). Dialectics provides the
'rational kernel' of the world outlook of the modern
proletariat. To become part of this outlook it must (in Marx's
famous comment) 'be turned right side up again'.[45] Yet nothing
could be more false than to see dialectics and idealism in Hegel
as accidentally connected, the *Logic* regrettably concealing its
light beneath a mystical bushel. Modern dialectics had, of
necessity, to develop out of an idealist critique of formalism; a
formalism carried to its logical conclusion in Kant's use of
'dialectic' to underwrite subjective idealism:

> Thus the antinomy of pure reason in its cosmological ideas
> vanishes when it is shown that it is merely dialectical, and that it
> is a conflict due to an illusion which arises from our applying to
> appearances that exist only in our representations . . . that
> idea of absolute totality which holds only as a condition of
> things in themselves . . . From this it then follows that
> appearances in general are nothing outside our
> representations—which is just what is meant by their
> transcendental identity.[46]

Hegel freed reason from its captivity within the Kantian
antinomies by the construction of an objective and systematic
science of dialectics in his *Logic*. But he could do this not by
any process of immediate extraction, either from nature itself
or from its reflection in the primitive, intuitive, dialectics of
Heraclitus. The task of construction required the elements to be
determined; that is, determined through negation of the
abstractions into which formal thought, regarding itself as
sovereign, had crystallised itself. A great self-confidence of
thought was necessary to rescue philosophy from its critical
state; a necessity negatively expressed in Hegel's description of
the way in which Kant imposed on philosophy

. . . a position which, while calling itself fear of error, makes itself known rather as fear of the truth.[47]

There would be, therefore, a certain light-mindedness in supposing that Hegel's idealism was a contingent defect, one which a more advanced thinker might have avoided, and which Marx in time corrected. Implicit in this view is the demand that Hegel should have constructed a new logic, while simultaneously depriving himself of the vantage-point within idealism from which he does so: what must be recognised is that the cunning of reason consists in knowing where to place the next step, not in taking both feet off the ground at once. There is a strenuous necessity contained within Marx's point (in the first of his 'Theses on Feuerbach') that

. . . it happened that the *active* side, in opposition to materialism, was developed by idealism—but only abstractly, since, of course, idealism does not know real sensuous activity as such.[48]

Materialist dialectics took its shape *within* the framework of idealism. As is normal with a foetus in the womb, it was 'standing on its head'. This should not conceal from us the fact that the main features of the child are already distinct, but neither should we confuse gestation with birth, or demand that the mother and the midwife be the same person.[49] At the conclusion of the *Science of Logic* Hegel returns to the correspondence between the stages in the history of philosophy, and the successive forms of the logical Idea. But, despite the fact that both versions of the Logic are sprinkled with asides about individual philosophers or philosophical schools, as exemplifying particular 'shapes' of the idea, Hegel makes no claim to have established an exact and comprehensive correspondence. Where a correspondence is claimed, it is frequently paralleled in a remark of the *History of Philosophy*: to Parmenides and the Eleatic school corresponds the opening phrase of the Logic proper, 'Being, pure being'[50] out of its negation in 'pure nothing', their 'immediate vanishing' one into the other, emerges for the first time a developed concept of 'becoming' in the maxims of Heraclitus;[51] in the Platonic idea Hegel sees thought (now conscious of its own distinctness) demand for the first time concrete objectivity of consideration—the knowledge of 'being for self' extracted from accident and contingency;[52] in Spinoza's unity of thought with extension as the attributes of substance (a unity which, because it is static, entails also an absolute opposition) he sees 'Actuality as the unity of essence and existence . . .'[53]

The fact, though, that a number of quite definite points of correspondence can be made does not imply that there is any overall 'mapping' between the development traced within the *History of Philosophy,* and the *Science of Logic*: even though a first glance at their structures might suggest it. Each work is divided into three major sections, of which the third represents in a very general sense the resolution of an opposition developed between the first two. In the *Science of Logic* both this triplicity and its own internal structure are represented in the arrangement of the work. It consists of two 'Volumes'. The first is itself divided into two 'Books', dealing with the 'Doctrine of Being' and the 'Doctrine of Essence' respectively, while the volume as a whole has the title 'The Objective Logic', which 'takes the place of former *metaphysics,* which was intended to be the scientific construction of the world in terms of *thoughts* alone.' (SL, 63). The final volume has the dual title 'Subjective Logic or the Doctrine of the Notion', 'which is to be regarded in the first instance simply as the third to *being* and *essence,* to the *immediate* and to *reflection . . .* it is their *foundation* and *truth* as the identity in which they are submerged and contained.' (SL, 577).

The schema of the *History of Philosophy* is also a triplicity. In it, also, there is a 'logical' progression—which is, at the same time, broadly a chronological one. However, the 'logical' relations are not the same as those in the Logic. Greek philosophy (Thales to Plotinus and the neo-platonists of the third century A.D.) 'does not yet have regard to the opposition between Being and Thought, but proceeds from the unconscious presupposition that Thought is also Being.' (HP, I, 107). This is superseded by the philosophy of the Middle Ages, in which the contribution of Christianity is to make thought individually distinct so that 'God may be realised and may realise Himself in the consciousness of individuals who are spirit and implicitly free.' (HP, III, 3). The final period ('Modern Philosophy'—from Bacon and Descartes onwards) is thus faced, like the subjective logic, with the task of encompassing thought and being, but in a different form. In fact Hegel goes so far as to claim that modern philosophy 'has the Notion as its ground.' (HP, I, 109). It must re-accomplish the unity of thought with being in face of a rupture which is thought's own doing:

> . . . modern philosophy is hence not a free and natural thought, because it has the opposition of thought and nature before it as a fact of which it is conscious. (HP, III, 161).

This sketch account makes there appear to be a closer correspondence than there is—at least in the sense that the final, 'synthetic' stage is concerned with the explicit genesis of the 'Notion'.

In fact, the positions allocated to particular philosophers frustrate the attempt to establish the correspondence exactly. For example, Hegel opens the subjective logic by pointing out that 'the Notion has substance for its immediate presupposition' (SL, 577) and that 'the philosophy which adopts the standpoint of *substance* and stops there is the system of Spinoza' (SL, 580) thus confining the essential significance of Spinoza to the second part of the Logic as a whole. But in the *History of Philosophy* Spinozism unquestionably falls in the third, modern, period, '. . . is related to the philosophy of Descartes as its necessary development only . . .' (HP, III, 220). There is another striking anomaly near the end of the objective logic. (SL, 536 *et.seq.*). Two consequences, says Hegel, follow from the indivisibility of Spinoza's substance, the first of which is 'that substance lacks the principle of personality—a defect which has been the main cause of hostility to Spinoza's system.'[54] This defect, Hegel goes on to argue, was put right—not by Christian metaphysics, but in Leibniz's monadology in which 'the principle of reflection-into-self or of *individuation* stands out as essential.'[55] Yet in the *History of Philosophy* this individuation of the absolute in the form of a personal God is the task of Christian philosophy of the Middle Ages, culminating in the Reformation as the 'absolute relation' of the pious individual to God. This logical 'anachronism' indicates something more general—that it is the sections of the *History of Philosophy* on Christianity which are least reflected in the *Science of Logic;* although the Logic is punctuated with assertions concerning the vital (even if secondary or ancillary) truths imparted by revealed religion, the definite parallels are much scarcer than with Greek or modern philosophy.

The *Phenomenology* does not by any means draw such extended parallels with the *History of Philosophy* as does the *Science of Logic.* When, in the final section ('Absolute Knowledge'), Hegel sketches the role of philosophical thought in the self-embodiment of consciousness, he concerns himself only with modern philosophy from Descartes to Schelling;[56] and he expressly contrasts it to (and regards it as superseding) religious reflection which '. . . has all the harder task in dealing with its essence, the content of its consciousness alien to itself.'[57] He even refers to the religious communion as a 'crude form of consciousness',[58] confirming the impression of an idealism that is, at heart, definitely secular.

Dialectic

But if the *History of Philosophy* does not, except in the broadest sense, find its own plan laid out in the *Science of Logic,* the Logic still provides the most complete exposition and justification of Hegel's dialectical method—a method of which the first deliveries of the lectures on the *History of Philosophy* represent, along with the *Phenomenology,* one of the earliest developed applications.

The core of Hegel's dialectics lies in his attack on the logic of the 'understanding' (as opposed to 'reason')—in particular on its crystallisations in the laws of non-contradiction and of the excluded middle. All things, Hegel insists, have become what they are and (in due course) they will also become what they are not. This fact is (as in several places he ironically remarks) not at all mysterious; on the contrary it is something to which perception and common-sense are, in practice, quite well accustomed. Nevertheless, this perception and common-sense coexist in the same consciousness with a systematisation of thought, a logic, which—for the sake of drawing clear and absolute distinctions—erects laws which can express the essence of things only so long as they continue to be what they were and do not become what they are not.

The logical systematisation of thought (whether or not it is consciously formulated) rules over thought's empirical judgments, tending to subordinate them to its own restrictions. As long as its laws are applicable, as long as the predicate asserted of the object by the judgment remains wholly correct, logic avoids collision with experience. Yet there remain crucial points at which the logic of the understanding is inapplicable and at which the claim that one, and only one, judgment regarding the object can be true and the other (its negation) must be absolutely false, itself leads to falsity. These are the points of transition, where an object is ceasing-to-be what it has been. At these points the old logic provides not a framework or a guide to judgment, but on the contrary a straitjacket. Accordingly Hegel makes the centrepiece of his 'reformed' logic the 'law of the unity of opposites'—the explicit denial of the law of non-contradiction. The intention is to express, within the idiom of the formal logic, the necessary conditions of becoming. This assertion of real contradiction forms the heart of the dialectics that is 'recognised as necessary to reason.' (SL, 831).

The dialectical character of the movement towards higher rationality is visible in the *History of Philosophy* in two senses. In the first place philosophical innovation or advance is explained as arising from the contradiction of doctrines or definitions within a given philosophical position or, occasionally, from a conflict between the subject's philosophical position and his actual relation to his world— though to give rise to a transition *within philosophy* this relation to the situation must find an expression within consciousness which comes into conflict with the claims of existing philosophical consciousness. Secondly, philosophy itself has flirted with or embraced dialectics in various pre-rational forms. It usually, Hegel says, (SL, 831-3) takes the form of asserting that some object has both a particular determination and its opposite. From this the most common conclusion is one of 'nullity'. But this nullity might take two forms—that the object itself is impossible, or that 'cognition is defective', and that dialectic is thus able to impose an illusion on it; often cognition 'flies into a passion, seeing in it [dialectic] perhaps a piece of sheer foolery, or, where morally important objects are concerned, an outrage that tries to unsettle what is essentially established and teaches how to supply wickedness with grounds.' (SL, 832).

The essential fault with this view lies in seeing dialectic as wholly negative, as eroding categories and philosophical determinations which already exist and which, but for interference, would have proved satisfactory for cognition. For philosophy to achieve itself as science its determinations must abandon their fixity and opposition; each must be deduced from the contradiction inherent within previous determinations.[59] Contradiction inheres, though, not only in opposite determinations of thought, maintained separate from each other and from their object, but where they actually unite and exist; that is, at the point of real alteration of actual objects.

Thus Hegel argues (SL, 830-1) that the method of philosophy is both analytic and synthetic: analytic since it needs to determine its categories as the negation of other categories; synthetic in that the absoluteness claimed by these determinations must itself be negated in the establishment of new determinations.

This unity of the analytic and synthetic is something that philosophic thought has in common with other forms of cognition; what distinguishes it is the way its determinations aspire always to absoluteness, requiring each dissolution and synthesis to approximate the rational and ordered form set out in the development of the *Logic*.

From this it would be possible to conclude that Hegel goes unambiguously in search of a purely rational impulse for the history of philosophy—yet at least two striking features of his exposition robustly contradict this. Within the last section of the subjective Logic, the first of its three elements is represented as Life,[60] the process which 'distinguished from its objectivity . . . pervades its objectivity and, as its own end, possesses its means in the objectivity and posits the latter as its means.'[61]

This might seem surprising in a work widely seen as an increasingly ethereal ascent into theological idealism. Hegel grants that 'if logic were to contain nothing but empty, dead forms of thought, there could be no mention in it at all of such a content as the Idea of Life',[62] but goes on to explain that the Idea ('the subject matter of logic') must at first 'be considered in its immediacy, it must be apprehended and cognised in this determinateness in which it is *life,* in order that its treatment shall not be an empty affair devoid of determinate content.'[63]

Not only the inclusion of 'Life' in the Logic, but its particular placing, has a definite significance. As the subject of the first chapter of the last section, it is by implication also the immediate form taken by the recapitulation of the forms of philosophical cognition within the third chapter ('The Absolute Idea'). The third chapter 'sublates' within itself the development of cognition, the 'elevation of the Notion above life' (SL, 775) as it attempts to render itself self-subsistent. From this one might quite reasonably draw the conclusion that the *History of Philosophy* paves the way for a return of philosophical thought into unity with life. And the second surprising fact is that such a supposition finds itself emphatically confirmed in the closing passage of the last lecture:

> It is my desire that this history of philosophy should contain for you a summons to grasp the spirit of the time, which is present in us by nature, and—each in his own place—consciously to bring it from its natural condition, i.e. from its lifeless seclusion, into the light of day. (HP, III, 553).

If Hegel may be accused of unreality, it is in failing to insist that life itself must be transformed before it can once again become inhabitable by philosophy.

Notes

[1]   *Lectures on the History of Philosophy* (trans. Haldane and Simson) (hereafter 'HP') 3 Volumes (1892-6). Sources of quotations from frequently-cited works of Hegel are abbreviated in parentheses; other sources are given in footnotes.

[2]   See *Phenomenology of Mind* (trans. Baillie, 1966) p 75.

[3]   Kaufmann, W., *Hegel: Reinterpretation, texts and commentary* (1966), p 11.

4   Findlay, J. N., *Hegel: a re-examination* (1962), p 339. The reference is to the 'three courses of lectures on Aesthetics, on the Philosophy of Religion and on the History of Philosophy'.

5   Heine, H. (trans. Snodgrass) *Religion and Philosophy in Germany: a fragment* (1882).

6   *ibid.,* p 153.

7   *ibid.,* p 152.

8   Marx, K. (trans. Nicolaus) *Grundrisse* (1973).

9   Lenin, V.I. (trans. Dutt) *Collected Works, Vol. 38* the *'Philosophical Notebooks')* (1963), pp 86-238.

10 He has suffered comparable neglect within bourgeois philosophy (particularly in England) during most of this century. The author of a widely-read undergraduate textbook in political philosophy opens his lengthy treatment of Hegel's political and social theories with the admission that it may be that the essence of the Hegelian metaphysic 'is beyond me, and I do not think I greatly mind if it is so.' (Plamenatz, J., *Man and Society* (1963), Vol. II, p 129). That it is no great distance from incomprehension to straightforward abuse is underlined by the title of a recent essay of Italian feminism *Sputiamo su Hegel* ('Let us spit on Hegel'), by Lonzi, C. (1970). Lonzi claims that 'the feminist issue places in question the whole work and thought of absolute man', (p 3).

11 *'The Logic'* from *The Encyclopaedia of the Philosophical Sciences* (hereafter 'EL') (trans. Wallace, 1968).

12 *Science of Logic* (hereafter 'SL') (trans: Miller, 1969).

13 See Harris, H.S. *Hegel's Development* (1972) and Plant, R. *Hegel* (1973).

14 *Theologische Jugendschriften* (Ed. Nohl and Mohr, 1907).

15 See Kaufmann *op. cit.* p 23-24.

16 See Guthrie, W.K.C, 'A History of Greek Philosophy' *Vol. 1: The Earlier Presocratics and the Pythagoreans,* p 70.

17 Novack, G. *The Origins of Materialism* (1965), p 84.

18 HP, I, 184.

19 This point is made by Guthrie *op. cit.,* p 65.

20 Novack, *op. cit.* p 90.

21 Hegel places Heraclitus chronologically as 'in part contemporaneous with Parmenides' (HP, I, 279). (The weight of recent opinion is that Parmenides was Heraclitus' junior, probably by about twenty-five years; see Guthrie *op. cit.,* p 408.) Hegel clearly sees the path of philosophic advance, though, as running from Parmenides to Heraclitus. The Marxist, George Thomson, takes the opposite view: that Heraclitus is merely the final expression of primitive dialectics, while Parmenides marks

the transition to an ideal 'substance'. (Thomson, G. 'Studies in Ancient Greek Society', Vol. II *The First Philosophers*, (1955), p 299-300). Ironically, Thomson implicitly disputes Hegel's own judgement of Heraclitus: '. . . whereas Hegelian dialectics represents that which is new and developing, the dialectics of Herakleitos represents that which is old and dying away.' (p 299).

22 Hegel makes the point explicitly at HP, I, 283.

23 Hegel attacks in particular (HP, I, 430) one of his own main sources for the *History of Philosophy*—Tennemann's *Geschichte der Philosophie*—for judging Socrates' condemnation 'revolting to humanity'.

24 Hegel (trans. Knox) *Philosophy of Right*, (1967). Hegel treats of the subjective preconditions of social freedom in paragraph 279. In a rider to the passage he explains the inadequacy of the Athenian constitution: 'It might be said that an organic, articulated constitution was present even in the beautiful democracy of Athens, and yet we cannot help noticing that the Greeks derived their final decisions from the observation of quite external phenomena such as oracles, the entrails of sacrificed animals, and the flight of birds . . . At that time, self-consciousness had not advanced to the abstraction of subjectivity, not even so far as to understand that, when a decision is to be made, an 'I will' must be pronounced by man himself'. (*Philosophy of Right*, p 288). In the body of the same paragraph, he explains how in Socrates 'we see the will which formerly had simply transferred itself beyond itself now beginning to apply itself to itself and so to recognise its own moral nature. This is the beginning of a self-knowing and so of a genuine freedom.' (p 184).

Hegel poses the matter similarly in a remark in the *Lectures on Fine Art* (trans. Knox, 1975) 'The subject wants to have the consciousness of being substantial in himself as subject, and therefore there arises in this freedom a new conflict between an end for the state and one for himself as an inherently free individual. Such a clash had already begun at the time of Socrates . . .' (Vol. I, p 510).

26 In the context of Socrates' criticism of Greek religion, Hegel inserts a justification of laws against blasphemy and subversion on the grounds that '. . . the State really rests on thought, and its existence depends on the sentiments of men, for it is a spiritual and not a physical kingdom.' (HP, I, 439).

27 'He . . . stands before us as one of those great plastic natures consistent through and through, such as we often see in those

times—resembling a perfect classical work of art which has brought itself to this height of perfection. Such individuals are not made, but have formed themselves into what they are.' (HP, I, 593). Earlier on Hegel remarks both that Socrates' father was a sculptor, and that Socrates himself may have worked as one. (HP, I, 389). A similar comparison is made in the *Lectures on Fine Art*. Socrates is pictured as one of those 'out-and-out artists by nature, ideal artists shaping themselves, individuals of a single cast, works of art standing there like immortal and deathless images of the gods.' (Vol. II, p 719).

28 *Phaedo* (trans. Tredennick, 1966).

29 These details of Hegel's early interest in Socrates are given in Harris, *op. cit.*, pp 14-16, 134.

30 Harris *op. cit.*, p 16.

31 'Tübingen fragment' of 1793 (translated in Harris *op. cit.*, p 488).

32 'The Positivity of the Christian Religion' in *Early Theological Writings*, p 82.

33 *Lectures on the Philosophy of Religion,* (3 Vols trans. Speirs and Burdon Sanderson, 1895), Vol. III, p 86.

34 Kant, living peacefully at Konigsburg, nonetheless eagerly read the newspapers on the development of the revolution in France (see Droz, J., *L'Allemagne et la Révolution Francaise* (1949), p 155), and in several passages expresses enthusiasm for its potential.

35 i.e. He is quick to anger.

36 See, for example, Marx, K. and Engels, F. *The German Ideology,* Part One (Ed. C.J. Arthur 1970), pp 97-100; and Marx, K. (trans. Moore and Aveling) *Capital,* 3 Vols, (1961), Vol. I, p. 20. (Marx's Afterword to the 2nd German edition.)

37 Heine, *op. cit.,* pp 108, 153.

38 Kant argues the inability of 'speculative reason' to prove the existence of God in *Critique of Pure Reason,* (trans. Kemp Smith, 1970), pp 499-524.

39 Kant I. *Critical Examination of Practical Reason,* in *Kant's Theory of Ethics* (trans. Abbott, 1889), p 222.

40 'The proposition that the finite is ideal constitutes idealism. The idealism of philosophy consists in nothing else than in recognising that the finite has no veritable being. Every philosophy is essentially an idealism or at least has idealism for its principle, and the question then is only how far this principle is actually carried out.' (SL, 155-156).

41 *Critique of Pure Reason* pp 504-506.

42 See 'Tübingen fragment' of 1793, cited above.

43   The passage in question follows on from a discussion of the Kantian antinomies.

44   Trotsky, speaking in exile in 1932, insisted on this future task of the rational reconstruction of consciousness: 'Human thought, descending to the bottom of its own psychic sources, must shed light on the most mysterious driving forces of the soul and subject them to reason and to will. Once he has done with the anarchic forces of his own society man will set to work on himself in the pestle and retort of the chemist. Mankind will regard itself as raw material, or at best as a physical and psychic semi-finished product. Socialism will mean a leap from the realm of necessity into the realm of freedom in this sense also, that the man of today, with all his contradictions and lack of harmony, will open the road for a new and happier race.' (Lecture in Copenhagen, *In Defence of The October Revolution,* London, n.d.)

45   *Capital,* Vol. I, p 20.

46   *Critique of Pure Reason,* pp 448-449.

47   *Phenomenology,* p 133.

48   Marx, K. 'Theses on Feuerbach' in *Selected Works* (Ed. Dutt, 1942), Vol. I, p 471.

49   This argument on the connection of dialectics with idealism in Hegel in no way supports the now fashionable opinion that dialectics *requires* idealism, and that consequently Hegel was consistent as against Engels and Lenin, piecemeal peddlers of a spurious 'dialectic materialism'. This account ignores Hegel's many analyses of dialectical development within the finite, reduces contradiction to paradox, and concludes (as Stedman-Jones, Engels and the End of Classical German Philosophy, *New Left Review,* No. 79, 1973, p 28) that, 'We can have materialism or we can have the general dialectical law of motion. But we cannot have both.' For other recent expositions of this view see Colletti *Marxism and Hegel* (1973), Coulter *Marxism and the Engels paradox* (in *The Socialist Register,* 1971), and Kolakowski *Marxism and Beyond* (1971).

50   'It was the Eleatics, above all Parmenides, who first enunciated the simple thought of *pure being* as the absolute and sole truth . . . in the surviving fragments of Parmenides this is enunciated with the pure enthusiasm of thought which has for the first time apprehended itself in its absolute abstraction.' (SL, 83). (See also EL, 160 and HP, I, 254 and 278).

51   'As the first concrete thought-term, Becoming is the first adequate vehicle of truth. In the history of philosophy, this stage of the logical Idea finds its analogue in the system of Heraclitus.

. . . [Heraclitus says:] Being no more is than not Being . . . a statement expressing the negativity of abstract Being, and its identity with not Being, as made explicit in Becoming: both abstractions being alike untenable. This may be looked at as an instance of the real refutation of one system by another. *To refute a philosophy is to exhibit the dialectical movement in its principle, and thus reduce it to a constituent member of a higher concrete form of the idea.'* (EL, 168, my emphasis). See also SL, 83. and HP, I, 283 *et. seq.*

52   '(Plato) does not understand by this a one-sided thought or, what is understood by the false idealism which makes thought once more step aside and contemplate itself . . . as in opposition to reality . . .' (HP, II, 1); and '. . . Plato demanded of cognition, that it should *consider things in and for themselves,* . . . that it should not stay away from them catching at circumstances, examples and comparisons, but should keep before it solely the things themselves and bring before consciousness what is immanent in them.' (SL, 830).

53   'Being is here more definitely regarded as extension; for in its abstraction it would be really only . . . that simple equality with itself, which constitutes thought. The pure thought of Spinoza is therefore not the simple universal of Plato, for it has likewise come to know the absolute opposition of Notion and Being. Taken as a whole, this constitutes the idea of Spinoza . . .' (HP, III, 257). See also SL, 536: 'Spinozism is a defective philosophy because in it reflection . . . is an *external thinking.* The substance of this system is *one* substance, one indivisible totality . . .' (Emphasis in original.)

54   SL, 537; the reference is to accusations of pantheism against Spinoza.

55   SL, 540. See also p 162 on the essential *self*-relation of the monad.

56   *Phenomenology,* pp 802-803.

57   *Phenomenology,* p 802.

58   *Phenomenology,* p 801.

59   'Thus all the oppositions that are assumed as fixed, as for example finite and infinite, individual and universal, are not in contradiction through, say, an external connection; on the contrary, as an examination of their nature has shown, they are in and for themselves a transition; the synthesis and the subject in which they appear is the product of their Notion's own reflection. If a consideration that ignores the Notion stops short at their external relationship, isolates them and leaves them as fixed

presuppositions, it is the Notion, on the contary, that keeps them steadily in view, moves them as their soul and brings out their dialectic.' (SL, 833).

60 Section 3 of the Subjective Logic ('The Idea') is divided into Chapter 1: Life, Chapter 2: The Idea of Cognition, Chapter 3: The Absolute Idea.

61 SL 760. Hegel sketches in this section a development within life: from the living individual, through the life process, to the being of the genus.

62 SL, p 761.

63 SL, p 762.

INDEX